Cyber Guerilla

Cyber Guerilla

Jelle van Haaster

Rickey Gevers

Martijn Sprengers

ELSEVIER

AMSTERDAM • BOSTON • HEIDELBERG • LONDON
NEW YORK • OXFORD • PARIS • SAN DIEGO
SAN FRANCISCO • SINGAPORE • SYDNEY • TOKYO
Syngress is an imprint of Elsevier

SYNGRESS.

Syngress is an imprint of Elsevier
50 Hampshire Street, 5th Floor, Cambridge, MA 02139, United States

British Library Cataloguing-in-Publication Data
A catalogue record for this book is available from the British Library

Library of Congress Cataloging-in-Publication Data
A catalog record for this book is available from the Library of Congress

ISBN: 978-0-12-805197-9

For information on all Syngress publications
visit our website at https://www.elsevier.com/

www.elsevier.com • www.bookaid.org

Publisher: Todd Green
Acquisition Editor: Chris Katsaropoulos
Editorial Project Manager: Anna Valutkevich
Project Manager: Priya Kumaraguruparan
Designer: Mark Rogers

Typeset by Thomson Digital

Contents

About the Authors

Jelle van Haaster, LL.M. University Utrecht, BA War Studies, Faculty of Military Sciences, is an award-winning writer, software programmer/developer, and speaker. He is an officer in the Royal Netherlands Army and has a diverse background in legal, military, and technical defense matters. Jelle recently developed an award-winning software app for effectively utilizing social media during military operations, and he is the author of multiple scholarly IT-Law, IT, and military-operational publications. He is currently completing his multidisciplinary PhD thesis on the future utility of military Cyber Operations during conflicts at the Netherlands Defense Academy and University of Amsterdam.

Rickey Gevers is currently Chief Intelligence Officer at the security firm Redsocks. He has been responsible for numerous revelations regarding high-profile security incidents both national and international. He was, amongst others, the first person to discover key logger used by Dutch law enforcement agencies and uncovered several criminal gangs and their operations. As an expert in technical matters he has been frequently consulted or hired as lead investigator, including in some of the largest security incidents the world has ever seen. Rickey appears frequently in Dutch media and has hosted his own TV show called *Hackers*.

Martijn Sprengers is an IT security advisor and professional penetration tester who is specialised in conducting covert cyber operations, also called "red teaming". He performs digital threat actor simulation by using real world tactics and techniques to infiltrate complex IT environments for his clients. With his vast knowledge of offensive security he helps international organisations to strengthen their preventive security measures, increase their detection capabilities and prepare themselves for real attacks. He holds an MSc in computer security, performed research on password encryption techniques and has written multiple articles in the field of IT security, cybercrime, and cryptography.

Foreword

In the days of yore, an occupying force only had to worry about other occupying forces, thus focusing their efforts on defensive posture. As internal conflicts loomed, and guerilla forces began to strike in unilateral and seemingly decentralized movement, occupiers realized their greatest weakness—that their enemy was within.

During *Guerre d'Algérie* (1954–62), French forces found themselves stumped by the effectiveness of the initial wave of guerilla style warfare across Algeria. Although outnumbering their counterparts, *Front de Libération Nationale* (FLN), The French found themselves in a conundrum: give up its occupied territory or eliminate the threat. They chose the latter and won the battle, but lost the war by means of popular opinion. Whether by design or coincidence, French forces were seen as aggressive and abusive in their response, and FLN reached the goal they had set from the beginning: *Libération*.

With the conceptualization and implementation of the Internet came a new era of warfare. Being able to communicate with people around the world at will changes the defense scope and methodology. While the French forces had to deal with and understand an enemy which was confined within a border, security forces now have to deal with and understand an enemy that claims none. The Arab Spring started on the streets of Sidi Bouzid, Tunisia, but spread like wildfire across social media. The power of the people, and its information propagation, toppled governments and hierarchies.

Attribution becomes nearly impossible as attackers adapt with every failed mission, evolving their tactics and combining their experiences as groups meet and merge. It only takes a team of 4–10 to cripple an infrastructure if members are designated roles, where each member can independently focus on their strong points and research is combined. From information gathering and reconnaissance, to exploit development and social engineering, they continue to expand on attack methodologies while defensive forces struggle to keep up.

Alas, the era of the cyber guerillas.

"Hold out baits to entice the enemy. Feign disorder, and crush him."—Sun Tzu

Hector Monsegur ("Sabu")

Preface

Conflict used to be about borders. A long time ago, we would defend ourselves by living in cities surrounded by walls. Those walls kept enemies away. Over time, the walls around cities become higher, longer, and wider. The longer and wider these walls, the more invisible they became, marking areas of wealth, prosperity, power, and belief systems. Eventually, those walls became borders. And, for hundreds of years, conflict was about borders. Conflicts were about conquering land or converting people from their belief system to another belief system.

Conflict and war have always been fueled by technology. Technology like gunpowder, steel blades, and fighter jets. The staggering possibilities of technology always seem to shine at their strongest during periods of war. War has been a real driver of technology. And technology has driven war.

One of the side effects of the Cold War was that the Internet was created. The US military created it as a way to uphold a chain of command during nuclear war. The Internet was created as a military infrastructure. By developing the Internet, mankind opened up a whole new way of waging war on one another. And, the Internet has no geography. It has no borders. By creating the Internet, mankind opened up a Pandora's box where tangible borders and recognizable enemies ceased to exist.

In addition, war used to be symmetric: armies would fight other armies. Technology of war has moved on. We no longer know, nor can clearly describe, who the enemy is, what they want to achieve, or what their motives are. We go into battle using technologies we do not fully understand, against enemies that remain in the shadows, and into wars that we will never know whether or not they are over. Who is the enemy? Hackers? Anonymous? The Russian Mafia? North Korea? Islamic State?

Cyber guerilla distills the conviction that smaller forces can rival larger forces in influence in our networked society. And, cyber guerilla is a perfect example of what asymmetric conflict looks like today.

Mikko Hypponen
Chief Research Officer, F-Secure
Helsinki, Finland.
Jan. 8, 2016

Introduction

Have you ever realized that the rise of information technology has enabled the individual more than any other entity? Most would probably answer "no" or "I do not know," which is only logical considering the current impetus emphasizing the dangers of networking and information technologies. States have seized the information technology domain as a new way of monitoring and controlling citizens—all for the sake of peace and security.

A domain aimed at the free, unhindered flow of data is quickly becoming the proving ground for States. The Internet has been dubbed a new warfighting domain, a battlespace that is proving to be the host of most 21st century conflict. Conflicts that will revolve around influencing others through information, about creating, collecting, controlling, denying, disrupting, or destroying that information.

A cyber prefix flood has securitized every aspect of information technology, white papers have earmarked cyber systems, cyber citizens, cyber threats, and many more as part of the cyber environment. William Gibson's pristine cyberspace—coined in his 1984 book *Neuromancer*—has become militarized, spawning a new breed of military action dichotomized as cyber war, cyber attacks, and cyber operations. As the whole domain is claimed by States, one would indeed almost forget that it is the individual who is most powerful.

But, what role can a mere individual play on the stage set by States? Most publications focus on means and methods available to States, how States should organize their cyber forces, govern their cyber infrastructure, conduct cyber operations, etc. As States are the focal point of those publications, one could step into the pitfall of overlooking the vast amount of options open to an individual. An individual on its own or in unison with like-minded individuals can influence equally or even more effectively than a State.

Feeding the construct that the individual is the least powerful actor in cyberspace is the practice of information security "professionals." They characterize actors using arbitrary parameters as advanced persistent threat, organized crime, insider threat, hacktivist, and script kiddies/noobs. These types of actors have varying skill sets, training, and experience, and potential impact. By doing so, information security professionals disqualify the place of a noninformation security individual or less knowledgeable practitioners on a stage set by States. They tend to equate potential influence to information security training and knowledge. This is, however, nonsensical—the capacities at an individual's disposal are unparalleled compared to the means at the disposal of information security professionals a decade ago. The noninformation security individuals have a vast array of capacities at their disposal; these are just a click away. Individuals only have to tap into these vast resources to claim their rightful place on the stage.

There are many technical manuals and how-tos showing individuals how to use specific cyber and information technology capabilities. This is in sharp contrast with the few publications aimed at illustrating how to generally and effectively utilize cyberspace with these capabilities;

in other words: Focus on the bigger picture. Tools and capacities alone are not enough to become influential in cyberspace—first, organization, strategy, tactics, and shared convictions are required. This book is one of the rare publications *also* aimed at these elements. It will, among others, touch upon tools, tactics, and procedures but it will also look at the bigger picture. This book is about showing that the individual can match the power of States, (large) corporations, and any other actors. Its purpose is to provide a counterweight to the current push toward emphasizing the power of States and large actors over individuals. At the same time, this book, *Cyber Guerilla*, will function as a warning to these actors believing that they reign supreme in cyberspace and on the Internet.

This book will provide a comprehensive description of cyber guerilla; it will cover this subject doctrinally, organizationally, and technically. Chapter 1 will describe the theoretical and ideological foundations of cyber guerilla. As such, it will serve as a doctrinal prelude to Chapters 2 and 3. Chapter 2 will focus on the cornerstone of cyber guerilla: the hacker group and its members. As cyber guerilla requires a versatile, intelligent, and very specific type of individual to fight on the digital forefront, this chapter will discuss the organizational aspects of the hacker group but also other aspects such as mind- and skill-set. After having described the conceptual and organizational foundations, Chapter 3 will focus on the tactics, tools, and procedures with which cyber guerilla is fought. Lastly, this book will look at illustrative State and non-State hacker groups and draw lessons from their activities in Chapter 4. The last part of Chapter 4 will consider the consequences of future developments on cyber guerilla, hacker groups and their tactics, tools, and procedures.

Jelle van Haaster

Chapter

1

General principles of cyber guerilla

J. van Haaster

■ INTRODUCTION

This chapter will describe the theoretical and ideological foundations of cyber guerilla. As such, it will serve as a doctrinal prelude to the organizational Chapter 2 and the technical Chapter 3. Part 1 of this chapter will describe the essence of cyber guerilla and how it differs from conventional guerilla. After describing the essence of cyber guerilla, Part 2 will show concrete footholds for formulating a clear (end-)goal and strategy for the hacker group. When the hacker group has clear goals and a coherent strategy, it can start conducting activities to achieve the goals. Although cyber guerilla shares similarities with conventional guerilla on a conceptual level, the tactics differ considerably. Part 3 will highlight the fundamental characteristics of cyber guerilla tactics: asymmetry, mobility, and stealth. As with any strategy, operation, or tactic, it should be tailored to the situation at hand. As Che Guevara made clear, a situation can favor the guerilla or the opponent. This is the same during cyber guerilla; there are favorable and unfavorable circumstances. Part 4 will describe circumstances favoring cyber guerillas and Part 5 will expand on unfavorable circumstances.

THE ESSENCE OF CYBER GUERILLA

What is cyber guerilla but another phrase feeding the cyber prefix flood? The simple answer: cyber guerilla is but an idea. Cyber guerilla is a conviction that smaller forces can rival larger forces in our networked society. Whereas Guerilla Warfare is a specific way of waging asymmetrical war in a specific situation against a conventional army, cyber guerilla is more universal. Cyber guerilla is waged not only in times of struggle, political unrest, or during conflict, this type of guerilla is also a way of engaging actors in peaceful circumstances as a form of protest, very much like electronic or cyber civil disobedience. Whereas cyber civil disobedience is always a nonviolent, disruptive type of protest, cyber guerilla has an amorphous character. In times of struggle, political unrest, or conflict it may take a violent and disruptive form, whereas in peaceful circumstances it may mirror the character of civil disobedience. The character of cyber guerilla will depend on the situation at hand, the strategy of the hacker group, and the context of the operation.

Cyber guerilla, unlike guerilla warfare, is not a prelude to ultimately becoming a conventional actor, to attain enough momentum within the population to be able to field an army. As such, it is narrower in scope than guerilla warfare, which is about overthrowing and replacing the State. Whereas cyber guerilla tactics alone can contribute to revolution, they cannot achieve physical revolution on their own. Cyber guerilla tactics can influence the masses and serve as a primer for these types of change, but the change itself requires some form of physical action. Apart from the ultimate goal of guerilla warfare—becoming a State actor—the goals are very similar to those of cyber guerilla.

Cyber guerilla is also about attaining momentum. Like Che Guevara's traditional guerilla band, the hacker group waging cyber guerilla starts off with a base of like-minded individuals aimed at making themselves heard. Just like gaining momentum for fielding an army and overthrowing larger actors in a conventional guerilla, the hacker group requires momentum to be effective and reach its goals. Lacking support or attention of the media and the masses will prove to be the end of any attempt of a hacker group to maximize their potential. Such an unpopular hacker group may be able to affect the State and other actors via cyber guerilla tactics, but as these actions are standalone and lack support they will be "just another hacker collective." To make themselves truly heard they require the masses and (social) media to amplify their effect.

The viability of a cyber guerilla is derived from the hacker group's potential, which consists of the ability to gain popular support and the ability of group members to conduct operations. These members, the cyber guerillas, are the ones at the virtual frontlines, the ones conducting the operations. Understanding their motivations will further understanding of the hacker group. There are many different motivations for joining or creating such a group; some are very similar to the motivations of a conventional guerilla fighter: as a form of protest against an oppressing actor and to protect others from this oppression. Oppression in this day and age may still entail physical oppression, but far more likely is intellectual, creative, social, and informational oppression. Cyber guerilla fighters dedicate themselves to influencing actors engaging in such oppressive activities. Guerillas do so on their own terms, on the terrain where these oppressive actors feel safe but can be hurt most, at times when these actors are least aware, and at the places they least expect. Cyber guerillas are only capable of doing so when they have intricate knowledge of the domain: the Internet and associated information systems. They need to know ways of circumventing safeguards; accessing and infiltrating networks and machines; exfiltrating information; how to manipulate the users and their supervisors; and how to sell the operations to the masses. These knowledgeable members form the nucleus of a hacker group; they can attract and educate new members and start to establish their strategy.

CYBER GUERILLA STRATEGY

"War is always a struggle in which each contender tries to annihilate the other. Besides using force, they will have recourse to all possible tricks and stratagems to achieve the goal." Che Guevara's statement rang true for the best part of the 20th century and keeps its value in the 21st century. War has been replaced by terms such as conflict, hybrid war, war amongst the people, low-intensity engagements, (counter)insurgencies, and many more. What has remained the same and will be the same for the considerable future is the use of force and using all possible tactics and strategies besides force to achieve goals. These nonforceful means and methods are increasingly overshadowing classical uses of force in effectiveness and efficacy. Cyber guerilla encompasses a subset of these nonforceful means and methods, namely the means and methods making use of the Internet (or cyberspace) and information systems. Although these means are nonforceful in nature because they stem from a virtual domain (the Internet), they can have a forceful effect. These nonforceful means and methods are used to achieve a hacker group's goal or end-state. How to utilize these means and methods to attain a specific goal is epitomized in strategy. A hacker group should formulate one or more end-states and a strategy; these will ensure maximum effectivity of these means and methods vis-à-vis a specific opponent.

Strategy itself is not about how to use means and methods to achieve a specific goal (those are tactics). Whereas for many hacker collectives the action is the goal itself, those waging cyber guerilla see actions or operations as sequential steps to achieving an end-state: as means to an end. That being said, the hacker group should take time to formulate the ultimate goal or end-state and plan the strategy leading up to that goal. As the hacker group is most likely to be the smaller actor with fewer resources at their disposal, it is vital that an end-state and strategy is formulated. The group will not be able to bring down or influence the opposing actor instantly; there are sequential steps in achieving the end-state: the plan for reaching the end-state is the strategy.

A clear end-state is required before being able to formulate strategy; there should be no doubt why the hacker group exists and what it tries to achieve. The ultimate goal should be formulated in such a way that it is—to some extent—specific, attainable, and realistic while at the same time sufficiently generic. For instance, "influencing opposing actor A" is too generic; a better goal would be "make actor A stop infringing on personal freedoms". Influence is too generic and does not offer starting points for establishing strategy, whereas making an actor stop doing something is still generic but outlines the specific issue area the group wants to affect. The end-state is the why and what of the hacker group (why they exist and what they are trying to do); strategy is the how: how the hacker group can reach the end-state.

Strategy is about long-term planning, about the analysis of (partial) objectives, taking into account the situation at the time, and the ultimate goal. The situation at the time can only be understood by knowing oneself, the opposing actor, and the context. Assessing the hacker group in terms of strengths and weaknesses is a first step in understanding oneself. Issues that could be taken into account are training, education, logistics, readiness, and willingness of individual members and the group as a whole. After analyzing the hacker group, one can turn to the opposing actor: What are his strengths and weaknesses? Understanding the opposing actor involves analyzing his goals, strategy for achieving these goals, and resources at his disposal (eg, leadership capacity, popular support, financial means, informational means, etc.). As the action taken by the hacker group and the opposing actor does not take place in splendid isolation, it is paramount to understand the societal context of these activities.

The context at the time affects the effectivity of actions and reactions—people perceive an action from their personal context (eg, biases, prejudices, and feelings) and the societal context. A hacker group should be aware of these contexts as these can have a great impact on the effectivity of an operation.

For instance, when trying to influence a bank's dishonest decision makers for whatever reason, one might consider conducting a (distributed) denial of service attack against the network infrastructure, rendering online banking inoperable. Such an action may be perceived as criminal or malicious as the hacker group targets the common man wishing to use his banking service. Although this operation might be technically successful, it can be disastrous as far as effectivity is concerned; the hacker group may lose support and alienate the people. A hacker group that is aware of the context would decide differently, for instance by targeting the dishonest decision makers themselves, via a spear phishing campaign, and exploiting the information gained to slander the decision makers. Such an action may be hailed as benevolent and the hacker group may be seen as a champion of the common man against forms of injustice.

When a hacker group understands itself, its opponents, and the context, it can start to formulate strategy. Different end-states require different strategies, and as groups, opponents, and context are diverse there is no general rule for creating a strategy. As a consequence, a strategy can comprise virtually anything that enables the hacker group to achieve the desired end-state. Depending on how ambitious the end-state is, the strategy may have many objectives, partial objectives, and milestones in it.

CYBER GUERILLA TACTICS

Strategy is about aligning the efforts of the hacker group; tactics are about conducting the operations leading to achievement of the (partial) objectives. Tactics are on a much lower level than strategy; they are about the actual usage of the resources at a hacker group's disposal. Strategy and tactics should work in tandem. Without strategy a hacker group's activities are conducted inconsistently and randomly—a group without tactics will have big ideas but no activities. Like the character of cyber guerilla itself, cyber guerilla tactics are amorphous; they adapt to the situation at hand. Tactics depend on the desired end-state, strategy, societal context, and resources at a hacker group's disposal. The chapter on operations will discuss tactics in depth and breadth from a technical perspective. This part will highlight the three fundamental characteristics of cyber guerilla tactics: asymmetry, mobility, and stealth.

The first fundamental characteristic of cyber guerilla tactics is asymmetry. Cyber guerilla in most cases is about rivaling a conventional opponent with more resources—in other words the resource balance is asymmetric. The hacker group and the opponent have unequal access to resources; the opponent has easier access and more resources. This opponent cannot be defeated or manipulated if met on a level playing field as there would be one inevitable outcome for the hacker group: defeat. Hence, cyber guerillas resort to asymmetric means and methods. These are aimed at offsetting the imbalance in resources between the guerillas and the intended target. Asymmetric means and methods are aimed at and make use of the weak spots of the intended target, where the access to resources does not matter. By using this type of means and methods the imbalance in resources can be countered.

The second principle of cyber guerilla tactics is flexibility. Flexibility revolves around being able to constantly adapt to the situation at hand, before, during, and after conducting operations. Hacker groups should adapt quickly, strike swiftly, and move out rapidly, reducing the potential of being caught. Cyber guerillas should never try to face the opponent head-to-head, that is, unless the other actor has been attrited to such an extent that success is certain. Cyber guerillas should do everything to prevent being pinned in a certain physical or nonphysical location; they should be able to adapt flexibly and evade any attempt of the opponent to meet head-on. When cyber guerillas are pinned down, the bigger actor can focus his resources and manpower on that specific area. This will unavoidably result in an ineffective operation and have severe repercussions for the guerillas engaged in the operations. Therefore, cyber guerillas should operate in flexible, amorphous, mobile formations.

Stealth is the third principle of cyber guerilla tactics. Stealth is essential for hacker groups from inception of the hacker group to the conduct of operations and long after that. At the start of cyber guerilla, hacker groups need time to come up with a end-goal, strategy for achieving this goal, and organize all other aspects of the hacker group. In this planning stage cyber guerillas are very vulnerable—they have yet to conduct operations but they are communicating about their intentions to take part in these activities. Hence, they should take great care to avoid their communication being overheard or intercepted by others.

Stealth remains of utmost importance during the stages in which the hacker group conducts operations. The only exception is operations aimed at exposure of the hacker group or the opponent, but even then the hacker group should take care not to give away too much information regarding their group. In all other cases hacker groups are far more likely to keep the initiative and be successful when making sure that all feasible measures are taken to obfuscate the identity of group members, group composition, and the means and methods used during operations. Should the group fail to do so, they allow the opponent to wield the resources at their disposal to bring down the hacker group. Thus, during all stages of operations the hacker group should take care not to give away information unnecessarily.

Even after an operation has been executed successfully, stealth remains important. A hacker group may decide to draw attention to their success and take to the media. Whereas this can be very effective in most cases to exploit the success, it is not always the most optimal course of action. The hacker group should make a conscious decision to seek exposure and decide upon the risks and benefits of doing so. The hacker group also should be able to handle the (media) attention if it decides to take to the media. This means having members on standby to answer media inquiries, that is, spokespersons, and having decided the message which will be communicated via these spokespersons.

CYBER WARFARE ON FAVORABLE TERRAIN (WHEN TO WAGE GUERILLA)

In military doctrine there are two important concepts which were also used in Che Guevara's book *Guerilla Warfare*, namely: favorable and unfavorable terrain. Favorable terrain is the situation in which the optimal conditions for a guerilla are present, in other words, favoring the hacker group. In a classical sense this could comprise terrain providing cover for troops and support of the population. Unfavorable terrain is the situation where conditions are far from optimal and favor the opponent, such as open fields, no cover, and lacking support of the population.

As cyber guerilla takes place in informationized society, and not in mountains, forests, and fields as conventional guerilla, one might conclude that these concepts are not relevant to the hacker group. However, just like strategy and tactics, these concepts are vital to comprehend the context in which the hacker group operates and derive a modus operandi from that. The situation can favor the hacker group or the opponent; hacker groups have to adjust to the situation at hand and have to adapt swiftly. The following section will describe circumstances favoring the hacker group by looking at the opponent, social circumstances (context), and the hacker group itself.

Even in the most optimal conditions, cyber guerillas will most likely face an opponent with more resources than the hacker group. This can be considered the baseline for any hacker group—the opponent dwarfs the group in manpower, equipment, finance, and access to legal means. As discussed in the section on "Cyber Guerilla Tactics," guerillas should use asymmetrical methods and mobility to counter the opponent. Being the smaller actor, guerillas might conclude that the situation favors the opponent; however, this is not necessarily so. Again, it is emphasized that guerillas always fight a bigger actor; this is the baseline. Certain circumstances in relation to the opponent can still favor the hacker group.

An optimal condition to start activities against a larger actor is when the opponent is neither aware of the hacker group nor aware of being a target itself for the hacker group. As the opponent is unaware, the hacker group can conduct operations without being actively countered by the opponent, which in the first stages of operations—considering the access to resources—would inevitably result in failure in reaching the hacker group's goals. An unaware opponent is also more likely to have a more lenient security policy and lessened security awareness within personnel and leadership. These are ideal circumstances for cyber guerillas to start their operations, which will be discussed in Chapter 3. As mentioned in the section on "Cyber guerilla strategy," stepping into the pitfall of only looking at the opponent will result in unsustainable operations; it is paramount to take into account the social circumstances or social context.

To make their cause truly heard, hacker groups require the support of the population. They can get support by mobilizing sentiment in favor of their cause, but the most optimal circumstance is when there are already sentiments within society benefiting the hacker group's goals. These sentiments may be caused by physical oppression, or intellectual, creative, social, and information oppression. These sentiments generally revolve around injustice, of a bigger actor harassing the smaller actor, the State versus the individual, the large company versus the common man, legislation favoring the few to the detriment of many, or the unrelenting effort to impede upon the freedoms bestowed upon Man. If these sentiments already live within society, the hacker group can adapt its tactics to the situation at hand. The hacker group can align itself with the forces already present within society and supplement these forces with operations in the digital domain. Aligning itself with sentiments within society should be done with a purpose—these sentiments should fit within the strategy of the hacker group and its goals. Should it contribute to the hacker group's strategy and goals, aligning itself with sentiments within society can contribute to support for the hacker group's cause.

The state of the hacker group itself also largely determines whether the situation favors the group or the intended target. An experienced hacker group, with a clear goal, strategy, aware of the societal context, and thought-through tactics is far more likely to achieve its intended goal than a group lacking all these. The situation is favorable if all aspects of the hacker group are thought out and taken care of; these include logistics, training, education, leadership, and tactics, tools, and procedures to be taken into account when conducting operations. Chapter 3 will cover how to organize these aspects on a group level. A group can have intricate plans, splendid organization, and still fail. A plan never survives the first contact with an opponent; hence, a hacker group should be able to flexibly adapt to changing circumstances. This requires knowledge, skills, and experience rather than detailed plans. It is about finding the right group members and empowering them to conduct operations. Chapter 2 will focus on these personal aspects of the hacker group composition.

CYBER WARFARE ON UNFAVORABLE TERRAIN

Unfortunately, in most cases the hacker group will find itself in less than optimal circumstances; in those cases the group should adapt to the situation and try to optimize conditions. When conducting operations in this type of unfavorable circumstances, one should be extra careful to uphold the three characteristics of cyber guerilla: asymmetry, flexibility, and stealth. Before being able to tailor the activities to the unfavorable situation the hacker group should be able to determine that the situation is indeed unfavorable. This section will describe how to appreciate the situation by discussing the opponent, the social context, and the hacker group itself.

Notwithstanding that guerillas will most often face an opponent with more resources—an unfavorable situation in itself—the situation is unfavorable when the opponent can wield these resources to counter the hacker group. The opponent can only do so when he is aware of the hacker group; he can only become aware if the hacker group breaks cover. There are plenty of good reasons for breaking cover, among others to improve one's position (eg, access escalation or moving to another geographical location), to conduct an operation aimed at exposure of the opponent or the hacker group itself, or to move to another (hiding) place. These reasons for breaking cover are not necessarily detrimental to the hacker group.

Accidentally being discovered when conducting an operation can have far-reaching negative effects on the group, whether in preparation, execution, or exfiltration phase. If the opponent or actors supporting their investigatory activities (eg, law enforcement, information security companies, computer emergency response teams) uncover an operation in progress, the opponent becomes aware of the hacker group. Only when the hacker group's operation is aimed at exposure is this type of awareness good; in most—if not all—other cases this will adversely affect the hacker group, its members, and their operations. The opponent can focus its efforts on a single entity, the hacker group. By doing so, the opponent flattens the playing field and can face the hacker group head-on, thus turning the asymmetrical situation into a symmetrical one.

There is no doubt that the opponent will win on an even playing field. Hence, the hacker group should observe the characteristics of cyber guerilla tactics: asymmetry, flexibility, and stealth. The group should do everything to prevent confronting the opponent head-on: Guerillas exploit asymmetrical means; these will be rendered useless if employed in a head-to-head situation. Should the unfortunate situation arise in which the latter situation is imminent, guerillas should observe the second characteristic: flexibility. The hacker group should try and move out of the focus of the opponent and their supporters or try to shift the focus to another area. The group can move out of the opponent's focus by moving their operations or base of operations to another location. Although much harder, a hacker group can try to shift the opponent's focus to another, more pressing issue area.

Cyber guerillas derive their support from the population; the population can have a supportive, neutral or opposing stance to the goal hacker group or lack any disposition regarding their issue areas. A supportive or neutral sentiment is favorable to the hacker group; by tailoring strategy, tactics, and operations to these sentiments, popular support can be increased and used to make operations more effective [see Cyber Warfare on Favorable Terrain (When to Wage Guerilla)]. Depending on the level of commitment and trust, supporters can be employed for tasks: for instance, helping to spread the hacker group message online and offline (least-trusted supporter), actively supporting operations (trusted supporter), and engaging fully in operations (confidant).

When the sentiment is opposing the hacker group or there is no sentiment regarding the specific issue area at all, the situation does not favor the hacker group. The hacker group, to be successful, will need to mobilize, create, or convert sentiment within the population. This will require considerable time, efforts, and manpower. Some might still wrongly argue that popular support is not necessary for operational success. This is true for the short term—the group might conduct actions and be successful at it without having a support base. The actions taken, however, will only have short-term effect on the lower, tactical level and a very limited foothold in people's minds and media (social and conventional). A more serious and thought-through approach to popular support is required to have success on operational and strategic levels.

If sentiment is lacking or opposing the goals of the hacker group, the group should consider using other, preferably related, issue areas to gain a foothold within the population. They can use these areas as stepping stones for mobilizing sentiment or converting negative sentiment. A powerful tool for claiming or (mis)using other issue areas for one's own message is framing. The essence of framing is that the form in which information is presented to a specific audience influences the impact and effectiveness of the message. Before being able to frame, the hacker group should be aware of the societal context and the target audience they wish to influence. Using messages tailored to specific groups using effective frames can have a profound effect on the support for the hacker group, its operations, and their goals. The Section "Media Strategy" (Chapter 3) will cover how to analyze the target group and methods for influencing the target group.

When the hacker group fails to take care of logistics, member training and education, leadership, tactics, tools, and procedures—any situation will be unfavorable to the hacker group. As hacker groups often are loosely organized, some might argue that this is the most effective modus operandi. This may be true in some cases, as with all organizational aspects of cyber guerilla: this depends on the context. There is, however, a very fine line between being loosely organized and not being organized and prepared. In the latter case the hacker group will face unnecessary risks and impede upon the effectiveness of operations.

Hacker groups are often claimed to be headless, that is, with a nonhierarchical leadership structure. We contend first that this is untrue and second that it would prove very ineffective for conducting operations. It is untrue as even within nonhierarchical networks some nodes are more important than others; in the case of the hacker group, some members have more knowledge, skill, or expertise and hence have a greater contribution to operations or the functioning of the group. Hacker groups are organized around knowledge, skill, and expertise—as such, they resemble a hierarchical network. This is the same for cyber guerillas organized in hacker groups; the nucleus of a group consists of the most knowledgeable members. For the outside world, however, the leadership structure of a group is unclear. The group might sometimes appear to be "headless" or nonhierarchical and in other cases a leader can be distinguished (often a spokesperson of the group).

Not using the more knowledgeable members and some form of hierarchy would result in chaos. The hacker group members making up the nucleus should fulfill a prominent role in recruiting and selecting new members, training and educating less-knowledgeable members, and planning (short- and long-term). They make up the informal leadership of the hacker group and should decide on logistics, member training and education, leadership, tactics, tools, and procedures. The hacker group may tailor its organization to the situation at hand—it may conclude that a loosely nonhierarchical organization may be best suited. A hacker group, however, has to make this choice consciously and not accept this type of organization as the de facto standard for hacker groups.

This section has covered how to recognize unfavorable circumstances for the hacker group by looking at the opponent, societal context, and hacker group itself. The exact modus operandi for the hacker group in a specific unfavorable situation cannot be described due to myriad possible contingencies. In any of these cases a hacker group should be aware of their disadvantage and try to improve their position. The hacker group should take greater care to uphold the characteristics of cyber guerilla tactics: asymmetry, mobility, and stealth.

CONCLUSIONS

In this chapter the foundations of cyber guerilla were described. Part 1 made it clear that cyber and conventional guerilla are similar in expressing that a smaller actor can rise up against a bigger and more powerful actor. Cyber guerilla, however, uses the means and methods of this time and differs in focus—it is not about becoming a conventional actor with a fielded army and/or overthrowing the State; it is about making an impact. Part 2 described how a hacker group, or those wishing to create a hacker group, should state a clear end-goal and derive a coherent strategy for achieving goals (Fig. 1.1). This strategy should encompass a plan for achieving the end-state by conducting operations (potentially containing many activities) using asymmetric means and methods, flexible formations, in a stealthy manner. Part 3 has discussed these three characteristics of cyber guerilla.

The three characteristics of cyber guerilla tractics are intrinsically linked and mutually enforcing. Using asymmetric means, aimed at different targets and via different venues of attack (flexibility) while making sure that no one notices (stealth), can have a great impact on the effectiveness of operations. Whether or not a hacker group upholds these characteristics can make a difference between being successful or being a mediocre and unsuccessful group. Parts 4 and 5 have exemplified circumstances that dictate the modus operandi for the hacker group, that is, favorable and unfavorable circumstances. In the former situation the group can operate in circumstances favoring the hacker group. The group composition is (near-)optimal and the group has room to conduct operations with less chance of the opponent or the population interfering. In unfavorable circumstances the group has less space to maneuver and a larger chance of being (actively) thwarted by the opponent, their supporting actors, and the population.

This chapter serves as a doctrinal/theoretical underpinning for a hacker group wishing to engage other actors during cyber guerilla. It is imperative

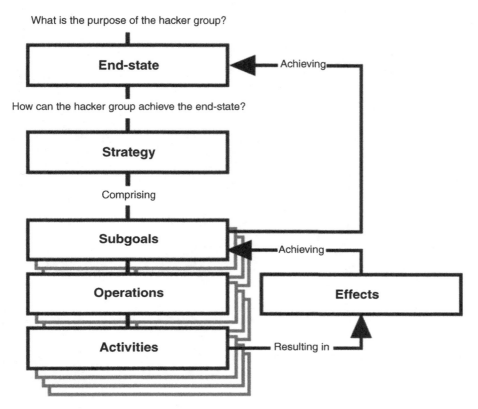

■ FIGURE 1.1   Overview of the process of creating a strategy and planning operations.

to understand these foundations to streamline the efforts of the hacker group in the short- and long term. Some might say that hacker groups, having a nonhierarchical or anarchical character, do not need (end-)goals, strategies, and tactics. This chapter has aimed to exemplify that a hacker group may do without these elements, but it will not succeed in making a lasting, long-term impact. Goals, strategy, and tactics help to streamline the efforts of different group members and make sure that all members know what they are in for and the purpose of the group. Chapter 2 will delve into the composition of the hacker group, the type of members sought after, and generally how to organize the group.

Chapter

2

The hacker group

R. Gevers

■ INTRODUCTION

Since the information revolution the Internet has been a driving force behind many—if not most—social reforms. From the 1% marches to the Arab Spring: The Internet was used to fuel, coordinate, and facilitate protests. The Internet turned out to be a safe haven for liberal thinkers and was used to establish contacts with other like-minded individuals at the other end of the globe. The global nature of the Internet makes (targeted) communication accessible to anyone. This was at the core of many great revelations: WikiLeaks being the first, The Intercept and Edward Snowden following quickly.

In the early days the Internet was a safe haven for free thinkers; there was no censorship and no laws were directly applicable. This opened up opportunities on the Internet to influence governments and their laws. However, this situation has changed: The Internet has become securitized and militarized. Whereas the Internet used to be a place aimed at free and unhindered flow of information and ideas, now it is increasingly influenced by State actors and large non-State actors. Whereas any individual could tread onto the Internet and fight for a cause, nowadays you need to tread carefully.

Chapter 1 has described the essence of cyber guerilla strategy, tactics, and the concepts of favorable and unfavorable terrain. In other words, Chapter 1 has laid out the overarching conceptual framework for cyber guerilla. As mentioned in Chapter 1, cyber guerilla is amorphous; it takes different forms depending on societal context. It may take a nonviolent form, resembling electronic civil disobedience, or a more violent, conventional guerilla-like form, albeit virtual.

These different contexts require a versatile, intelligent, and very specific type of individual to fight on the digital forefront. This chapter will zoom in to look at the cornerstone of cyber guerilla: the hacker group. Sections 1 and 2 will focus on the two roles hacker group members have to be able to fulfill. Mirroring the amorphous character of cyber guerilla, group members should be able to fulfill the role of (1) social reformer and (2) combatant. These two sections are aimed at describing the ideological foundations of hacker group members. Section 3 describes the hacker group composition and will describe the intellectual capacities and skill-sets needed in the group.

THE HACKER AS SOCIAL REFORMER

Anyone wishing to make a stand against a larger actor will ask himself what type of persons are sought after when organizing a hacker group. The type of person sought after can best be described as a social reformer, strongly developed in both intellectual and ideological sense. This person shares the firm belief that traditional laws do not apply to the Internet and the borders that sovereign rulers try to impose on the Internet are irrelevant. Although most political leaders will try to bring their laws onto the Internet, he believes that they will not succeed, in part because of his contribution to preventing them from doing so. He believes in the Internet as common good enabling the connection of communities and sharing information, knowledge, and ideas.

It should be stated that the Internet has enabled a borderless guerilla fighter. The territory of the cyber guerilla fighter is the borderless Internet. The Internet is the connecting element for fighters located in different territories. As a consequence of the global character of the Internet, new recruits can be found anywhere on the planet. This global character is reflected in the cyber guerilla fighter—he is a human being but, unlike many others, he does not feel bound by borders. Believing in a free, unhindered flow of information and ideas, he is not interested in religion, ethnicity, and sexuality. Information, knowledge, and technology prevail over any these irrelevant aspects.

The Internet functions as brains and nerve system for the hacker group. The Internet enables the hacker group to tap into a vast resource of community knowledge (brains) and to direct action via myriads of channels (nerve system). As Internet access permeates the world, the potential recruiting ground increases and offers many more to join the fight against all forms of injustice. Cyber guerilla is not an exclusively Western phenomenon; as the domain is global, possible recruits can hail from anywhere. As Internet access is benefiting cyber guerilla, the guerilla fighter should always strive to enable Internet access to those being cut off, censored, or otherwise unable of reaching the Internet. Giving or restoring people's access will increase the amount of potential recruits and supporters.

The individual sought after strongly opposes Internet censorship and feels he should fight against this form of oppression. Although the battle for a free Internet has been long lost, there are many new opportunities to escape, evade, and counteract the scrutinous eyes of States, large corporations, and other actors. These means open to any individual will be discussed later on in this chapter and Chapter 3. Besides that, the individual fighting cyber guerilla believes that only the Internet can guard our freedom of conscience, which is the only thing that could further humanity technologically, culturally, and sociologically. This individual is not trying to achieve megalomaniac feats as saving the planet; instead he aims to improve the quality of life for all gradually.

THE HACKER AS COMBATANT

As States and large actors seized the information domain, they sought ways of influencing other actors. The hacker and his code turned out to be a very effective weapon on this virtual battleground. In the beginning of the Internet, monitoring was virtually nonexistent; hence, anyone with a little hacker skill could penetrate any of its chosen targets. Without getting caught, one could easily wander through the computers of NASA or visit AREA51 digitally. The many videos of old-school hackers penetrating army.mil server, filming it, and throwing it online are testament to this period in time where anybody could hack. Sadly enough, by virtue of intrusion detection systems going mainstream that age is over right now. To overcome access controls and all other safeguards, a very knowledgeable and skillful individual is needed.

These types of individuals are very scarce and are sought after by IT companies, armed forces, intelligence agencies, and large corporations. As anyone is looking after these individuals, knowledge and skill have become the prime criteria above all else. For once soldiers do not care about the hacker's physique, as long as they are capable of shutting down the enemy's air defense system. The hacker in a combatant role has proven to be very effective, able of influencing large corporations and States.

Stuxnet is one of the most prominent examples of the potency of hackers in State-to-State relations. Government-funded hackers created Stuxnet and released it to manipulate the Natanz centrifuge. Although heralding the state and its intelligence agencies as the victor, this success was achieved only by virtue of hackers. Another example affirming the role of the hacker on the world stage is Edward Snowden's revelations. The Snowden files uncovered a virtual arms race in the realm of digital and economic espionage. The means and methods used in this arms race are developed, maintained, and executed by hackers. These examples affirm the power of the Internet and information technologies, and the role of hackers on the world stage.

Not only do hackers play a potent role in the arena of State-to-State relations; they are a force to be reckoned with even in internal affairs. As the Arab Spring and many other smaller protests have shown, one of the most successful ways of spreading ideas is through social media. Many governments try to censor such platforms and try to impose controls on these platforms. Censorship and controls are easily overcome by hackers; they can help movements by training and educating the protesters in ways of circumventing censorship. Although no hacker is needed to start a movement, hackers can make sure that governments will not succeed in tampering with movements, impeding on their outreach and their effectiveness in general. Examples include overcoming domain name system (DNS) censorship in Turkey, the Arab Spring (Tunisia, among others), and censoring BlackBerry usage during London riots. As such, hacker skills contribute to movement success. Exponential growth has gotten a new dimension with the rise of the Internet and social media—the hacker is the maintenance engineer and champion.

In the past decade we have witnessed many hacker groups operating—whether in support of or against a State actor—from conflict zones. Conducting operations from areas that are subjected to armed violence requires a different mind-set and organization. When conducting cyber guerilla during armed struggles, whether inter- or intra-State, the hacker group has to be prepared for physical violence, detainment, prosecution, and abductions. Hacker group organization capabilities, and the different tasks should be prepared with the utmost care when preparing for operations during conflict. Hacker group leadership should play a prominent role to prepare the group for this daunting challenge.

Acting against State or non-State military or militant actors involves the hacker group becoming a potential target for these actors. These actors have shown the willingness to use deadly force against those engaged in cyber activities, for instance by bombing their homes and workplaces. Other activities are the detainment or abduction of members by State agents, all showing that military or militant actors will most likely choose to counter hacker operations with physical force rather than virtually. The hacker group should prepare for this contingency when taking on a role in armed conflict.

Some might feel that the hacker group will not be targeted by physical action. The following example will illustrate what a group might expect when conducting activities during armed struggles.[1] The means and methods militant or military actors will use against (hacker) groups become apparent when looking at the group "Raqqa is Being Slaughtered Silently" (or Raqqa_SL) in Syria. This group is spearheading the Syrian media campaign against Islamic State (IS) in Raqqa. This group primarily focused on the use of (social)media to unveil the monstrosities committed by IS. This particular group is conducting extremely difficult work in an extremely hostile environment. Several of its members have been killed, not only within the occupied area in Raqqa, but also in other countries (such as Turkey). This exemplifies that a virtual activity may result in physical repercussions; a group that is conducting operations or something as simple as providing media coverage for the world to see have the risk of being killed.

The mind-set required is being prepared physically and morally for counterattacks by the opponent, not only virtual, but also physical attacks. When the hacker group is conducting operations that are hurting the opponent, the opponent will not shy away from drastic measures against the hacker group.

THE HACKER GROUP

The hacker group is the core of cyber guerilla and every operation undertaken. This section will describe the hacker group and its composition. The hacker group as a whole can exist out of numerous individual groups, but all should share the same goals. Operating as a whole of numerous individual groups should be, as mentioned in Chapter 1, a conscious choice of the leadership within a hacker group and depends on societal context, the opponent, and the state of the hacker group. To align the goals over different groups, a clear goal and strategy for achieving that goal should be formulated in the beginning stages of the hacker group. Whether there

---

[1]The authors are indebted to Guido Blaauw for writing this section on mindset required during conflict.

are multiple small groups or one large group, there are general tasks within hacker groups which should be taken care of. To be an effective hacker group, it is very important to specifically assign tasks to all individuals within the hacker group.

Disciplines

There is a variety of specific tasks within the hacker group; all of these tasks should be practiced with full dedication. Only in very specific cases can tasks be ignored as they are temporarily less relevant—for instance, the external communication discipline when establishing initial compromise. However, in most cases all of these disciplines should be fulfilled for the hacker group to succeed. The following sections will describe the different disciplines within a hacker group: leadership, infrastructure, internal communication, recruiting, engineering, forensics, command and control, development, and external communication.

Leadership

The core of the main hacker group should ideally consist of six individuals with one natural leader, but this is not a requirement and depends on the context of the operation. This nucleus is the leadership within a hacker group. The leader should be the one that spends most time online, is dominant by nature, but most importantly is able to understand all technical aspects of an operation. The leader of the hacker group should be verbally strong and possess strong technical skills.

The hacker group and its members are very vulnerable to egoism; members may decide to engage in operations for their own gain instead of trying to achieve the goal of the hacker group. Hackers are very vulnerable to getting caught up in their love for using and exploiting technology. To counteract this drive during an operation, the leadership should always keep the goal in mind and never let members of the group do anything else than their previously determined task. Becoming domain admin might be rewarding, but it is not always the goal of the operation and may result in unwanted attention. Conducting these types of unplanned tasks could compromise the whole operation and endanger all members engaged in the operations.

Besides keeping track of the hacker group's goals and progress in achieving these, leadership should also be vigilant of potential leaks within the hacker group (moles or snitches). In some cases hacker group members may be recruited by an opposing actor (law enforcement, other hacker groups, criminal organizations). The leadership should evaluate the loyalty of all members of the hacker group on a continuous basis. To prevent the leadership from being corrupted, one should not be able to easily join the core of the hacker group.

There are several guidelines with regard to the leadership structure within a hacker group. The pivotal points in the leadership structure revolve around 6 and 12 members An ideal group consists of 6 core members; whenever this group becomes more than 12 members the leadership structure has to be reconsidered and restructured. When considering restructuring it is best to apply a layered structure. Every layer should have its own degree of security and trust. The top layer, the six core members, should have the most stringent controls, safeguards, and precautionary measures in place. Should the group grow even further, new levels can be added to incorporate new members; these new members should be added to the bottom peripheries of the organization. Come time and once proven to be trustworthy, they can gradually climb within the organization.

Infrastructure

Another distinct set of tasks within the hacker group is infrastructure acquisition and maintenance. The ideal choice of infrastructure differs per operation; those responsible for planning and conducting operations should determine which type is suitable. There are many options with regard to infrastructure, all with specific advantages and risks. These aspects should be carefully assessed and evaluated in choosing specific infrastructure. Aspects to be taken into account are, among others, reliability, uptime, bandwidth, and interception possibilities. The following sections will describe different types of infrastructure and their advantages and risks. Note that this infrastructure is the attack platform for the hacker group but can also be used for communication and anonymity.

Hacked infrastructure

Hacked infrastructure is the infrastructure available to a hacker group as a result of obtaining control over infrastructure via hacking. The main benefit of using hacked infrastructure is that it is free. If the hacker group lacks sufficient funding, using hacked infrastructure can be an outcome. Using hacked infrastructure also has many downsides. The hacked computers will go down very quickly; often hacked server do not last longer than a maximum of 2 months. It is essential to know different types of infrastructure which can be hacked; the following sections will describe virtual private servers (VPS), dedicated servers, and shared web-hosting servers.

Shared web server. Shared web-hosting servers are the least beneficial. They are very easy to hack, but as it is easy to hack a shared web-hosting server, the hacker group is often not the only one hacking the server. Apart from the weak access controls, shared web hosting often has bandwidth limits in place; running out of bandwidth will result in the website going down. The bandwidth of a shared hosting web server is often low; hence they offer a very limited advantage to a hacker group. Another downside is the tendency of shared web servers to notify the owner of a website when the website runs out of resources; this could compromise ongoing operations of the hacker group. Apart from weak access controls and notifications to the owner, another downside of shared web servers is that some are maintained almost daily by system administrators. This means dedicated system administrators login on a daily basis to perform actions on the servers (eg, upload content, inspect logs, monitor bandwidth, look at analytics, etc.). These system administrators can be assumed capable of spotting hackers. This, again, could compromise the operation and cause unwanted attention.

Virtual private server. VPSs can be very useful as they often have good bandwidth and are not maintained on a daily basis. The problem here is the fact that VPSs often still have bandwidth limits. Once the server runs out of bandwidth, corrupting the operation, the owner of the website may be alerted. This could result in the hacker group's operation being compromised. Apart from running out of resources, the owner may also be alerted by the monthly bill, which may show extensive usage of the VPS.

Dedicated servers. Hacking a dedicated server can be very useful for the hacker group. Those are often the servers that perform just one task, have a default installation, and are not maintained on a daily basis. They usually have a big Internet connection because they are very important to the company owning them.

Higher bills at the end of the month because of increased bandwidth usage are often ignored and the bills are paid by the company because the server is that important to the company. If the hacker group decides to use a dedicated server as their main platform for reliable communication, it is recommended to run the server first for a few months and only after a few months decide upon switching. The first few months are the critical phase; if this server turns out to be stable during that time it will often stay online for a very long period of time.

Physical access infrastructure. Physical access infrastructure is the type of infrastructure which can only be used by physically moving to its location: for instance, war driving or accessing the network infrastructure at a McDonald's restaurant. This kind of infrastructure is not recommended. The infrastructure by itself is often unreliable, slow, monitored, and often heavily fire walled, let alone the possibility of surveillance cameras in the neighborhood capturing your presence. These networks can be useful though when very specific operations are going to be executed. This type of Internet access can be considered an extra layer of defense as it is geographically separated from the rest of the infrastructure of the hacker group. Some might ponder using the (wireless) network of neighbors. Using wireless Internet in the vicinity of a member's private residence is not recommended. Neighbors and other locals often know that someone is technologically proficient; any event relating to covert Internet activities will result in suspicion.

Infrastructure ordered with stolen credit cards

Infrastructure bought with stolen credit cards can be very useful. It provides the hacker group with the ability to use reliable infrastructure at a location of the buyer's choosing. Besides choice of location, buying a server will also make sure that the hacker group can select the server with the right disk space, processing capacity, bandwidth, management, and maintenance.

This type of infrastructure is ideal for a hacker group, for instance, if a hacker group would require a server to store large quantities of data extracted from a company as quickly as possible. One can choose a geographical location close to the hacked target and make sure the latency to the hacker target is as low as possible, making sure as much data as possible can be exfiltrated from the company in the least amount of time. Once the data are exfiltrated and put on this server it can be further spread to safer locations. After the need for the server is gone the server can be dismantled. Discovery of stolen credit card credentials is always imminent; this is the downside of purchasing infrastructure by using stolen cards. Eventually the credit card company will find out and revoke the credentials—this will most likely result in the hacker group's server shutting down. Luckily investigations into credit card misuse are rare; it is paramount, however, to be aware that the these types of activities can alert opponents and supporting actors.

Anonymously purchased infrastructure

Purchasing infrastructure anonymously is most ideal for creating long-term infrastructure (several years or more). Payments should be made anonymously, for instance through digital currencies relying on blockchain technology and prepaid credit cards. The hacker group should make sure that anonymous registration information is provided. Besides that, the hacker group should tread carefully in using the server, for instance the hacker group members should never login to any administration panel of the server from one's home server. This mistake is often made, that is, there are known cases of people contacting the hosting provider's helpdesk and signing off with their real name. This will result in operational comprise and severely impede the hacker group's operations.

Other assets

Apart from attack and communication infrastructure, there are other assets which might be obtained that are beneficial to the hacker group. The following section will list some of these assets and briefly describe their purpose and how to obtain them.

Code signing certificates. Code signing is a technique used mainly by the Windows operating system since their Vista version. The purpose of code signing is to detect whether someone is trying to illicitly tamper with the operating system. Before one can manipulate a Windows system driver, for example, the driver has to be signed. If an unsigned driver is used, several security precautions will be triggered. Therefore, it is recommended for the hacker group to be in possession of several code signing certificates.

Although people tend to think the process of obtaining a code signing certificate is difficult, in reality it is not. Developers tend to upload all their projects and code snippets to cloud storage solutions. As a consequence of the wide and careless use of these code signing certificates, there are a lot littered around the Web. Certificates can be found on Github, Pastebin, peer-to-peer networks, and online open directories. It is recommended for the hacker group to gather multiple certificates; they can obtain these from the aforementioned media.

Another way to get possession of certificates is to manipulate the certificate system; one can easily register fake companies and find online copies of identification documents that can be used to buy a code signing certificate. Buying your own code signing certificate gives the hacker group great control over the certificate itself, whereas using a stolen certificate offers fewer options and is primarily useful as an Easter egg. Which method of obtaining a code signing certificate is most beneficial to the hacker group depends on their operation.

VoIP servers. Voice over IP (VoIP) servers can be a great asset to a hacker group. Access to a VoIP server can help the hacker group to gain intelligence and to enable making VoIP calls under the guise of the company owning the VoIP server. Voice is still considered to be a very personal and direct way of communicating; trust is more easily established once a person's voice can be heard. As such, phone calls are still frequently used for social engineering activities. The hacker group can use VoIP servers for social engineering purposes but also to listen in on conversations taking place between employees (intelligence).

Obtaining VoIP servers can be very easy since there is an increasing amount of these servers around and many of those servers are improperly administered. Many of these servers are configured wrong, resulting in "open" servers, or not configured at all, resulting in "default" setting. Vulnerable VoIP servers are often listed on online vulnerability, exploit, and scan databases such as ShodanHQ. The hacker group could usurp the vulnerable servers, for instance, to listen in on conversations, use in social engineering, or internal and external communication.

Internal communication

An important task within the hacker group is providing communication for the hacker group itself. One or more members should be tasked to provide infrastructure and software to make communication easy and user-friendly. The infrastructure used to communicate must be run on dedicated hardware (see the section on infrastructure). This means that the infrastructure chosen to run the communication platform must be in full control of the hacker group and be completely trusted. Communication platforms are very vulnerable to wiretapping; hence, all communication within a hacker group should be encrypted.

The hacker group should further enforce strict procedures for accessing and using communication platforms. The hacker group should always keep in mind that every ACK packet sent—whether an RST or ACK,SYN—is registered and thus contains compromising information. Hence, when a hacker group chooses to use servers as their main communication channel, these should be made accessible only through The Onion Ring (TOR) network. This way the hacker group can guarantee that members, trainees, and other persons requiring access do not connect from their home addresses. Although taking precautionary measures, the hacker group should always be vigilant and never forget that servers are the most viable and useful for opponents and law enforcement agencies to tap. Therefore, the hacker group should make sure that everyone connecting to these devices is disciplined always to use encrypted communication channels.

The main communication platforms for hacker groups are TOR network, Internet Relay Chat (IRC), forums, and mobile messaging. The following sections will discuss certain elements to keep in mind when creating, maintaining, and administering these platforms.

The Onion Ring network

TOR network is the only network recommended for use by the hacker group. While initial communication and simple information gathering can be done without TOR, once operations are coming closer the hacker group should always switch wholly to communication over the TOR network. The reason for doing so is that the TOR network is the only network protecting your true physical location on the Internet. Besides that, it also offers safeguards against wiretapping. Apart from using the TOR network, the hacker group should always use other layer(s) of encryption to communicate, for instance run plain text through another cryptographic tool before sending it via the already encrypted communication channel.

Many hackers using TOR generally make one huge mistake: they install their TOR client on the same computer they perform operations with. This will result in unprotected network traffic when TOR client crashes or unexpectedly terminates. After crashing or termination, the running tool sets to search for a new connection; it will find one over the regular Internet connection. Another related problem could be data leakage due to wrongly configured programs that bypass the TOR network and set up their own connection, resulting in personally identifiable information leaks. Once this has happened log files at the target site can be used to determine the attacker and compromise their identity. This could cause operational failure and have severe repercussions for the safety of the hacker group.

The hacker group members should share best practices regarding optimal use of the TOR network and precautionary measures. It is essentially up to the hacker, however, to take appropriate measures to prevent Internet access if the TOR Internet connection goes down. This can be achieved in several ways. One of them is putting a tunneling device (for instance, a bridge or other dual-interfaced device) between the device that is being used to access Internet resources and the outward-facing Internet connection. Using this method, hacker group members can make sure all Internet traffic is routed onto the TOR network. Devices such as the Raspberry Pi can be used for this purpose; they are cheap ($80) and offer great value for the money.

Internet Relay Chat

Communication within the hacker group is often performed through IRC. Hackers tend to favor IRC as it is close to command line and easily script-able. Another reason hackers favor IRC is that it does not have specific disadvantages. As previously mentioned, the infrastructure to host the IRC channels on must be trusted. That being said, the hacker group should operate on the notion that the channel will be wiretapped. To thwart attempts to listen in on conversations, IRC provides many ways to encrypt its communication. It is up to the hacker group to enforce a strict policy of mandatory channel encryption. Preferably all channels should use its own scheme of encryption; there should never be a standardized predictable encryption scheme or reusage of passwords.

Wherever an ongoing campaign is coming to a climax the hacker group should always switch to a temporary server and channel. The hacker group member tasked with communication should facilitate this infrastructure and take care of its reliability and encryption. Not until the last moment should location and encryption details be communicated with all individuals joining the operation. Only when all members taking part in the operations have joined the channel should detailed information regarding the operation be communicated. Once the operation has been successful the server and channel should be left immediately. Details regarding the channel should be stored on a server that only a select number of individuals can access.

It is up to the hacker group to enforce a strict IRC channel policy—one of the elements needing discipline is posting links. This should be prohibited on both IRC and forum communication platforms since the chances of anyone accidentally revealing their identity by clicking on a (malicious) outbound link is too large. Although everyone knows not to click links and to mask their IP address, an individual of the group will click that link and will reveal its identity. Once the identity of one member of the hacker group is compromised, all hacker group members are in great danger. Therefore, links should always be forbidden and removed. Links can be replaced by a simple "hxxp" or "redacted," as long as they are never interpreted by any interpreter as existing links. The hacker group members should always educate and train each other on how to properly and consistently make use of technology to mask their true location on the Internet. Apart from that, hacker group members and leadership should also train and force members to change their online identities frequently. The use of digital sock puppets clouds the activities undertaken by members; not taking these precautionary measures may result in the member being profiled.

Apart from forum and IRC policy, the forums need to be built in such a way that they only allow TOR exit nodes to connect. Again, note that this does not result in perfect safety, as failing Transmission Control Protocol (TCP) connections will still be seen during a wiretap and will eventually compromise someone's identity. Hence, this type of communication should be used in lower-level channels, for instance in the channels used to educate trainees who are not yet employed in active campaigns.

Levels of trust
As mentioned previously in this chapter, a growing hacker group can consist of multiple layers of leadership and members. Within these layers different levels of trust and security apply (Fig. 2.1). Members that are new to the hacker group always enter through the level of lowest trust. It is up to

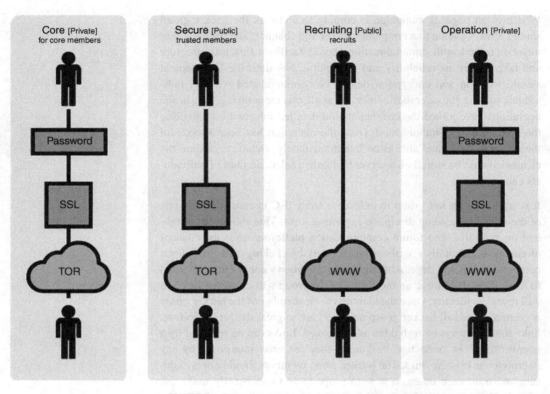

■ FIGURE 2.1 Example of a communication scheme with different means and methods for communicating.

the hacker group itself to decide upon the number of layers and criteria for moving between higher and lower layers. When considering criteria for moving up and down in the organization, the hacker group should keep in mind the purpose of the layered structure, namely, the ability to scale and more importantly slow down and mitigate the effects of infiltration attempts. Rising to the highest levels of the hacker group (the core at the top of the pyramid) should take long, as this is the highest level of trust. The member should been an active member; he should have been engaged in operations frequently and proven to be a trustworthy member.

Although it is of utmost importance to prevent covert agents from entering the core group, fear of such situations should never be leading when conducting operations. Fear will only cause panic and false accusations, ruining the morale within the group and generally reducing the effectiveness of the group since it is fighting itself instead of the opponent. The threat of infiltration is always present; taking basic safeguards, such as levels of trust and security, should dissuade most infiltrators or mitigate the impact of these individuals on the group.

Forums

Apart from IRC channels, the hacker group can decide on using forums as their primary communication channel. Most of the aspects discussed at IRC will also apply to forums; this section will highlight some additional points of interest. Should the hacker group decide to use a forum as its primary communication channel, once again infrastructure of the highest reliability grade should be chosen (see the section on infrastructure). The downside of using forums is that all messages are stored on a server and encryption is less useful. It is very easy to create very specific rules and regulations on a forum; this way trainees and recruits can be guided and protected closely. Forums can be very useful for spreading knowledge among members, trainees, and recruits, for instance, by posting instruction guides, how to's, instructional videos, and other useful informative posts.

Access to the forum should always be regulated. The forum should be structured to distinguish core members and new (potential) recruits that have restricted access to the forum. The parts recruits have access to should be those parts where they are able to showcase their skills and show their eligibility for the hacker group. Core members tasked with recruiting (see the section on recruiting) should keep a close watch on this channel. By looking at the conversations they can easily spot and differentiate between fraudsters and new promising members. As mentioned at IRC, compromising details (eg, information on operations, personally identifiable information, etc.) should never be posted on the forums.

Mobile phone messengers

The Snowden revelations regarding mass surveillance sparked a lively secure messaging ecosystem on mobile platforms. These so-called "secure messengers" on mobile phone platforms can be used to exchange information in a hacker group. There are, however, several things to be kept in mind. Mobile phones, especially smartphones, collect and transmit tremendous amounts of metadata. Using metadata, it is quite easy to forensically determine communication has taken place. Apart from that, it is also rather easy to generate insight about who was communicated, at what location, and how much data have been sent. These secure messengers may protect from mass surveillance; they do not, however, protect members against targeted surveillance. As such, a hacker group member should always be aware of the information communicated by using the mobile platform.

VPNs and CloudFlare

An increasing amount of people hide their online identity and location through virtual private networks (VPN). Services such as CloudFlare provide an extra layer of security. However, it is paramount to realize that using a VPN is not a silver bullet—hacker group members can still be profiled when using a VPN. As such, it is unwise to trust a VPN wholly for providing anonymity, secrecy, and security. Hacker group members should be aware that almost all VPN providers cooperate with law enforcement and other investigatory agencies. Most VPN providers keep logs of their users' activity. These logs provide law enforcement with extremely valuable information; these logs can potentially compromise hacker group members, supporters, and operations. Therefore, the hacker group should avoid using commercial VPN providers, even those that say they delete logs or do not keep logs.

Another widely used platform is CloudFlare. Although it might be beneficial to some users, the hacker group should avoid CloudFlare at all times. There are strong indications that all information being transferred over the CloudFlare network is intercepted and decrypted by investigatory agencies. As such, the hacker group should avoid using this popular service.

Unconventional means and methods

Besides the conventional tools such as TOR, IRC, forums, and websites there are many unconventional means for communicating. These are the types of means not specifically intended for communication but which can be used to send a message. One example is the use of tags (graffiti) in online multiplayer gaming to exchange information. Games such as Counterstrike enable users to create custom tags. Entering the same multiplayer session enables two persons to exchange information. Apart from that there are many other unconventional ways of communicating, for instance using steganography on images and sharing these on inconspicuous-looking online channels (eg, Instagram). Or using the comment boxes on popular websites for sharing information (eg, YouTube comment boxes). The number of potential channels is only limited by hacker group members' ingenuity and creativity.

Recruiting

The hacker group derives its strength from its members; as such, it should always be on the lookout to recruit new members. A member of the hacker group should be assigned specifically for this recruiting task. This recruiter is responsible for recruiting, selecting, and approving new members. The hacker group should put in place a very secure process for recruiting, assessing, training, and educating new recruits.

To someone who knows what to look for, it is easy to spot talented and promising recruits. One can never become a good hacker if experimenting with technology is not in their veins; apart from ideological and intellectual capacity this is one of the core characteristics defining a hacker. Note that hackers who destroy computers, extort, or steal property are not potentially interesting to the hacker group. These individuals have a financial motive and are not interesting for the hacker group that is trying to recruit dedicated and correctly motivated hackers.

Upcoming young hackers often hack a lot of machines, usually without getting caught; there are hardly any thorough investigations into computer hacking cases when there was no big theft. Recruiters should work closely with members responsible for infrastructure to find these types of intrusions on hacked infrastructure. The members in the hacker group tasked with acquiring new infrastructure can perform these types of forensic tasks on systems to spot previous intruders on the system.

Once the hacker group identifies a system that has already been comromised it is useless for further use but the system can be extremly valuable for recruiting purposes. Compromised computer systems should be passed on to group members skilled in computer forensics. This group should investigate the system and collect all possible information on the system. The group should report their findings back to the hacker group. Important aspects are the modus operandi of the compromise, tools used, and possibility to trace the individual.

If the hacker group finds an individual eligible for recruitment, his contact details should be gathered. Finding his contact details will not pose any problems as for the hacker group—it is second nature to track individuals on the Internet. The hacker group can then establish contact, which should be done carefully. No compromising details about the hacker group should be revealed on first contact. Contact should be established and expanded very carefully; the steps of becoming a trusted member should take place gradually. The recruit can be tempted to join and rewarded by the hacker group by giving infrastructure, since true prospects of the hacker group are more satisfied with CPU processing power than with cash.

Once infrastructure access is given to a hacker group prospect, the new recruit's skill can be evaluated by tracking his movements on the infrastructure. Attention should especially be paid to very young individuals, as they tend to be ignorant. Young individuals should preferably not take part in active operations. The newly recruited youngsters should be adopted by the hacker group but only be put into action at a later moment, preferably years after recruitment. The fresh recruit often turns out to possess a number of entry points into systems that can be used for an operation. The recruit's entry points can be transferred to the hacker group and the hacker group can than appoint the right person to perform lateral movement (which will be discussed in Chapter 3). If an entry point of a fresh recruit is used, this recruit should completely transfer his entry point to the hacker group.

No backdoor should be allowed on the entry point provided by the recruit. The more senior hacker group members should carefully check for the existence of backdoors. If a backdoor is found, the loyalty of the fresh recruit can be put into discussion and his position should be reevaluated. If the recruit did transfer his compromise without a backdoor being persistent the recruit should be awarded. The award could for instance comprise technical knowledge (eg, regarding malware or other software) or processing power (eg, on servers).

Once the hacker group has performed the lateral movements starting from the entry point, the hacker who performed these tasks should have a conversation with the recruit. The more senior hacker group member should explain what he did and what the catch turned out to be. All of the movements done by the hacker should be explained in full detail, with full care, and no knowledge should be withheld. This way the recruit receives valuable information for his own good and trust is being established between him and the hacker group. The recruit will feel acknowledged, his entry points are appreciated, and he receives valuable knowledge for his efforts.

Engineering

Apart from the supporting tasks such as infrastructure, recruiting, and communication, the hacker group logically also comprises hackers/engineers. These are the ones dedicated to conducting the actual operations and are highly proficient in their specific fields. There are particular types of hackers/engineers sought after by the hacker group; we will now describe these types and the different disciplines.

The producer

The producer is a very proficient engineer with his own toolset. This type of hacker is required to create entry points and maintain persistence in targeted objects. He is characterized as having a lot of patience and always being eager to work. For this person programming is a lifestyle, hobby, and often professional occupation. This person is extremely skilled in programming, usually in one specific language. Multiple languages can be an added benefit but are absolutely not necessary for eligibility to join the hacker group.

Of particular interest are persons familiar with reverse engineering or programming add-ons for the Windows operating system. Having thorough understanding of the most-used operating system is a skill that often turns out extremely useful once the hacker group gets stuck at a specifically targeted system. The hacker group can then discuss the problem with the producer and often it will turn out this engineer has the solution to the problem, either in his own toolset or in his extensive knowledge of the operating system.

The viral growth engineer

The viral growth hacker/engineer is characterized as being capable of generating an extremely high volume of compromises. Where many familiar with computers can hack a machine with known exploits, this type of hacker/engineer is talented in a very specific way—he can achieve viral growth. Creating this type of growth requires a skilled and dedicated person. As many now how to create viral growth in theory, many feel that this is an easy task. Bringing this theory into practice, however, is completely different from theorizing about it. It takes a very specific talent to be able to create viral growth in practice.

The viral growth engineer/hacker is capable of achieving viral growth and has proven their ability of doing so. This person does not necessarily have to be as skilled as the producer, as long as he is able to achieve exponential growth. Most often this requires a mixed skill-set comprising social (engineering) and programming skills. Of particular interest are those engineers/hackers that have created viral growth with very common tools (eg, remote administration toolkits).

The creative hacker/engineer

The creative hacker/engineer is a very specific individual as well. He is highly interested in hacking and vulnerabilities; the only difference is that this person knows how to bundle and exploit vulnerabilities in such a way that it improves the effectiveness of known vulnerabilities. For instance, this person can turn a cross-site scripting vulnerability into remote code execution, and this person can bundle unchecked uploads in combination with remote file inclusion into a remote code execution. This is the engineer to which a hacker group should resort to find out-of-the-box solutions for targeting a system. While not being the quickest or most proficient programmer, using sheer creativity this type of hacker/engineer will find the solution to the problem. This hacker/engineer is not known by his awesome programming skills, but by his ad hoc scripts, which have a tendency to always work. Once a goal (target) is set, this is the person who achieves the goal one way or the other.

Forensics

Although forensics might not sound like a particularly relevant discipline to a hacker group, it can be very helpful for a variety of purposes, for instance recruiting, obfuscation, and intelligence. As such, having a member proficient in digital forensics is essential. As he is proficient in forensics, this hacker group member can provide the hacker group with feedback on using particular code or software. He can easily pinpoint mistakes often made while coding, using malware and advice on minimizing forensic traces. He also knows the modus operandi of forensic researchers and thus knows how to thwart investigations.

Although in the ideal world malware would not leave a single trace, we live in a far from ideal world in which malware always leaves traces. As such, the hacker group should prioritize suggested improvements to reduce the forensic imprint—knowing that investing too much time in trying to reduce the forensic footprint would be infeasible and ineffective. An exception to this practice is leaving easter eggs, ludic clues as to the (fake) identity of the perpetrator, to demoralize or mislead the opposing actor and to prove that the system has been compromised. Besides consulting the forensics member beforehand, this member should also be one of the first to take a look at a hacked target system after initial compromise. He can easily spot mistakes the initial hacker has made and can try or advise on taking precautionary measures or to wipe any residual traces leading to the hacker group.

Besides using the forensics discipline to improve the hacker group's operations, forensics can also gain valuable information from compromised systems. Forensics can, for instance, spot the presence of any other hackers on the system. As mentioned before, spotting another hacker on a target system can be one of the prime resources for new recruits. Although it may sound farfetched, in practice this happens quite often. Should the hacker group find another, nonmember hacker on the system, they should first try to establish why the hacker is on the system and how he has entered. Once the available information is analyzed, the hacker group should decide on establishing contact with the hacker or not. If the hacker proves not eligible for recruitment, the hacker group should still decide on what to do with him as he might compromise the goal of the operation.

One option would be to leave the hacker in the zone he is in; this should only be done if the hacker group has no time or other circumstances do not permit the second option: removing the unknown hacker from the target system. The best course of action upon finding a nonrecruitable hacker is removing him from the network and moving on. This does not mean that the unknown hacker cannot be contacted at a later moment, for instance when the hacker group hits a dead end and requires the hacker's knowledge (and entry points). The hacker group should never disclose the operation to the unknown, noneligible hacker as it might compromise the ongoing operation.

The unknown individual could become selfish and claim the compromise for himself, prove to be an informant or hunting team, or otherwise be detrimental to the operational success of the hacker group.

Should the hacker group feel that the hacker found on a system could be eligible for recruitment, contact should be established in a careful manner. First contact should always be careful; a simple "hello, we are …, who are you?" can be enough to break the ice. Once the hacker group has established that the hacker is not a threat to the hacker group or the operations, it is best to disclose general details on the operation to gain trust. Establishing contact with hackers already present in systems can be of crucial importance to achieve operational success. Since like-minded individuals with knowledge of target systems are rare, the hacker group should carefully consider turning down such an asset; in most cases it is a quick way of recruiting knowledgeable like-minded hackers.

Command and control

Command and control infrastructure should be put in place to exchange or exfiltrate information, manage (attack) infrastructure, and other issues requiring synchronization. Choosing the right command and control infrastructure for an operation can contribute greatly to operational success. Not thinking thoroughly about the command and control infrastructure or misconfigure the infrastructure can compromise the operation and the hacker group.

Data exfiltration

Ideally the command and control infrastructure uses TOR to hide its true physical location. However, the downside of TOR is that the connection often is unreliable and slow. Exchanging merely 1 GB of data can prove to be an excruciatingly slow process; due to connection timeouts and other interruptions one might end up transferring 8 GB just to exfiltrate 1 GB of data. Failing connections increase bandwidth usage and therefore increase detection possibility due to anomalies in network usage. To decrease the fail rate and increase the extraction speed, the ideal setup for command and control infrastructure is setting up as close to the target as possible (Fig. 2.2). The latency between the command and control server should be as low as possible and the Internet connection of the target should be carefully tested to determine the maximum exfiltration speed possible.

If the hacker group is aware of network monitoring tools being present in the network, they should carefully consider the extraction speed and rate. Preferably they should limit (or "cap") the speed to prevent network anomalies from taking place—both volume spikes and dips. The spikes may stand

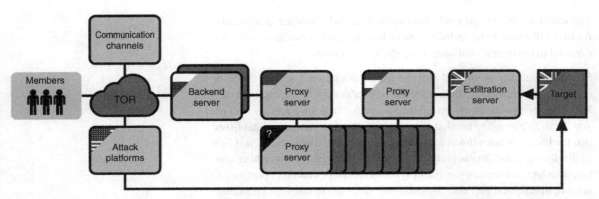

■ **FIGURE 2.2** Example of an infrastructure configuration required for operations.

out against normal network traffic, raising suspicion within network administrators. The dips may be noticed by legitimate users as exfiltrating at maximum speed may slow down the network speed for other traffic. The hacker group should carefully determine how to best prevent both spikes and dips while at the same time exfiltrating information as fast as possible.

Call backs

There are many types of malware that need to call back to the hacker group's command and control infrastructure, for instance to exchange data, receive updates, obtain instructions, or any other type of communication. The malware left on the systems should connect to an address that can be resolved via the DNS. Peer-to-peer could be considered, but it should be kept in mind that peer-to-peer traffic can be easily spotted on a network.

Malware planted on systems could contain domain names and backup domain names. If backup domains are used it is recommended to use different registrars in different jurisdictions to prevent effective coordinated takedowns. Another approach is to continuously download new backup domain lists. The new gTLDs are an outcome as well; the organizations operating these new TLDs are often new to the business and therefore lack connections and abuse departments. This is ideal to keep your domain online as long as possible.

Another way of keeping command and control infrastructure or systems running longer is using fast flux domains. The hacker group should, however, keep in mind that when transferring large amounts of data this does not provide an extra layer of security—the endpoint will be easily detected.

Domains should always be registered anonymously; some TLDs require business licenses or identification. It is very easy for the hacker group to obtain business licenses or fake identification papers that could be used to purchase these domain names. Once a domain name or server is purchased, the hacker group should be aware that the registrar shares all information with third parties. From the moment you register, Google's and other search engine's crawlers will start to index the domain. Therefore, the domain should be the last thing to be registered; first the other infrastructure should be put in place and appropriate security measures taken.

A mistake that is often made is attaching static infrastructure to the domain name to check if everything functions before conducting an operation. The hacker group should be aware that all IP addresses connecting to the domain are logged and available for later requests. All IP addresses ever attached to a domain end up in databases that are accessible for forensic researchers. These databases often provide extremely valuable information regarding the identification of hackers.

Proxies

The hacker group should always use a layered proxy setup (Fig. 2.2). The first proxy server should be the server closest to the target. This server basically serves as a relay server. Once data gets onto this server they are (ideally) forwarded to multiple locations. The benefit of this server is that there is no need for a speed limitation and therefore a server should be chosen with maximum bandwidth capacity. This relay server is the first server to be taken down if the operation gets discovered; hence the hacker group should aim to reduce the amount of data stored on this server. This can be achieved by forwarding exfiltrated data as quickly as possible to another proxy server or a backend server.

It is best for the hacker group to use disposable infrastructure. Ideally infrastructure should not be reused; after an operation the hacker group should dispose the used infrastructure. Members tasked with forensics should make sure the infrastructure is forensically wiped or at least aim to reduce traces. When considering the location of infrastructure, including proxy servers, the hacker group should try making investigation as hard as possible. One of the most effective things to frustrate investigations is using infrastructure from different legislation. To maximize the effort needed to investigate, the hacker group should preferably select Countries with completely incompatible legal systems or Countries that do not get along well. One can imagine, for instance, that a request for assistance from the United States of America to Russia takes longer to satisfy than one from the United States to the United Kingdom. The longer this time-frame can be stretched, the better for the hacker group.

Backend server

The backend server is the most important server during the whole operation (Fig. 2.2). This server can be one or more servers, depending on the operation. This server is used by the hacker group for collecting, curating, and analyzing retrieved data. To do this as fast as possible, backend servers should ideally have enough memory and especially disk space. To prevent data loss, the hacker group can consider creating a backup of the backend server, possibly offline.

Developers

Developers play a crucial role within the hacker group. The difference between a hacker and a developer is that the hacker creates "quick and dirty" tools while the developer takes more time to create a near-perfect tool which may be reused. It takes a lot of time, however, to develop effective tools that can be used by the group's hackers or engineers. In some cases, when operational circumstances permit more preparation time, the hacker group can task developers with building tools. Ideally the hackers instruct the developers and specify their requirements; the developer should then translate these needs into efficient tools.

External communication

Members tasked with external communication are the ones responsible for creating content for the various external communication channels maintained by the hacker group. As there are many possible channels using different media, this discipline will most likely be fulfilled by multiple members with a specific skill or one very skilled creative designer (eg, video editing, web design, illustration skills, etc.). Most essential for the hacker group is to have a skilled web designer capable of creating visually and technologically sound websites. This member masters languages like PHP, ASP, Ruby on Rails, CSS, Java, and most importantly HTML. The web designer is of utmost importance to a hacker group for creating and maintaining appealing communication channels—for instance websites. Besides building a website this member can be used to design other content for social media and forums. He can also be used to create phishing mails and websites or other content needing to be visually tailored to a specific target.

Press relations

The press relations (PR) subdiscipline of external communications is aimed at furthering the hacker group's goal by mobilizing support for the hacker group and denying support to opposing actors. The member(s) tasked with PR should maintain contacts with conventional press and maintain a firm foothold on social media. Of course, it depends on the context whether it is viable to use social media, conventional media, or both. The use of media will be exemplified further in Chapter 3 (media strategy). This section will, however, emphasize an essential activity for PR discipline: maintain contacts with reporters.

Reporters should be picked with utmost care since they can make or break an operation. The hacker group should carefully select a trusted base of reporters and establish a relation with them. These reporters can be selected on basis of their mind-set and audience, for instance activist journalists or neutral journalists with a large audience. Once there is a level of trust between a reporter and the hacker group, the relation can be enhanced by awarding the reporter with scoops and insider information. By doing so, a trust relation and mutual dependence will be established, which can be very extremely valuable to the hacker group. The value and impact of these types of cooperation become apparent when considering the mutually reinforcing relation between Edward Snowden and Glenn Greenwald.

The hacker group should aim to keep the trusted reporter base up to date regarding their operations, of course, only when exposure is beneficial to the hacker group. To keep them updated, they can be invited into communication channels (eg, IRC) or send an information package regarding a successful operation. By giving the reporter access to information, he will evaluate the newsworthiness of the content and could probably assist in creating a "product" that is more newsworthy.

CONCLUSIONS

This chapter has discussed the type of individual and mind-set required to conduct cyber guerilla. It has discussed the intellectual and ideological capacities a cyber guerilla should possess, best characterized as the hacker as social reformer and combatant. After that it has focused on the organizational aspects of the hacker group and distinguished various disciplines for conducting operations. Skillful and motivated group members and efficient organization enable the hacker group to conduct operations. The following chapter will offer the hacker group concrete footholds for conducting operations.

Chapter 3

Organization of #operations

M. Sprengers and J. van Haaster

■ INTRODUCTION

This book has discussed the concepts overarching cyber guerilla (Chapter 1) and the type of individual and organization required to wage cyber guerilla (Chapter 2). In line with hacker group practice, we have named the activities conducted by the hacker group members to attain their end-goal "operations". These comprise the activities resulting in an effect that, when successful, may contribute to achieving the end-goal of the hacker group. This chapter will describe activities preceding, during, and after operations. It is paramount to realize that in doing so, this chapter will cover only a select number of tactics, techniques and procedures (TTPs) available to hacker group members. Depending on the context and end-goal of the hacker group there are many other TTPs available to members for achieving a (end-)goal. Hence, this chapter should be seen as an illustrative selection of TTPs which may be employed when conducting operations.

This chapter will first describe precautionary measures to be taken before conducting operations, to prevent being profiled by opposing actors. After that, this chapter will turn to operations; the second section will cover the various stages of operations and consider the best TTPs during each stage. After having discussed the stages of operations, this chapter will cover the effects which can be attained with different operations and activities. As exposure and media can be an integral part of operations, this chapter will discuss media strategy fourth. Lastly, this chapter will touch upon post operational activities and discuss the possibilities open to the hacker group when they have reached their end-goal.

INTELLIGENCE

Intelligence comprises various notions, we will describe it from a counterintelligence perspective. This includes (1) counterintelligence in general and (2) counterintelligence during the conduct of operations. This section will first describe how to prevent being profiled (counterintelligence) and second how organizations gather security event information.

Counterintelligence in general

One of the most important aspects of a successful operation is the necessity of not drawing attention. The moment a hacker group has raised suspicion or has been profiled, the more complicated it becomes to operate stealthily and achieve their goals. To determine what precautions must be taken and what measures must be implemented to prevent detection of the operations, it is important to understand how the targeted organization(s) and possibly other investigative bodies try to perform their intelligence gathering and how they implement their detective measures.

Many counterintelligence and law enforcement agencies are involved in fighting digital operations and cyber intrusions. As such, the guerilla band can also become a subject of investigation. Although little knowledge is available on how most law enforcement agencies deal with cyber attacks, it is generally known that the moment that these investigative bodies can connect a digital identity to a natural person or group, they can easily be tracked and caught. For example, if the true identity of a (digital) suspect is revealed, these agencies can use more traditional means (such as physical posting, direct communications tapping, property searching, and interrogating) to investigate possible involvement in offensive cyber operations. Therefore, it is of utmost importance that the guerilla band ensures that their physical identities remain secret.

For a hacker group it is important to understand how counterintelligence generally is performed. Many counterintelligence strategies are based on some form of profiling, targeting, tasking, and action. In the end, the workload for the counterintelligence agency to identify the guerillas should be disproportional to the reward or value of a successful identification. For example, it is disproportional for an investigative body to establish a multimillion dollar operation to identify a 16-year-old kid who performs digital vandalism by attacking web shops, thereby causing damage for "only" $10,000.

In general, the following profiling levels can be distinguished:

1. Known identity, known risk. The counterintelligence body has determined the risk for specific identities, such as groups or individuals. The identities can be actively monitored (eg, through watch lists).
2. Known identity, unknown risk. The counterintelligence body has determined that specific identities might form a risk, but the risk is unknown. It will perform (automatic) monitoring based on profiles and indicators of risk.
3. Unknown identity, unknown risk. Both the risk and identity are unknown. Therefore, the counterintelligence should perform manual profiling to determine either one of the two. This method is logically the least cost effective.

It goes without saying that the guerilla band ensures they remain in the third group (unknown identity, unknown risk).

If the hacker group is growing quickly and has performed multiple (successful) campaigns and cyber operations, there is another profiling risk it has to deal with: *stylometry*. Counterintelligence bodies can fingerprint specific campaigns and determine (code) patterns and signatures, for example, the means and methods used, to determine if a cyber operation was conducted by the same hacker group. To decrease the probability of stylometry, the guerilla band should ensure that they implement strict guidelines with respect to initiating, executing, and finishing offensive operations. These guidelines should at least cover procedures for programming malware, methods to perform reconnaissance, usage of tools, geographical distribution, and leaving digital fingerprints. For instance, if a programmer makes the same coding errors, he can be identified in subsequent attacks. A real-world example is a hacker group which used attacks that matched the work hours in the Moscow time zone and the Russian holiday schedule.

Counterintelligence during operations

While executing cyber operations it is important to understand that every digital touch (of a system, a network, or a computer) leaves some form of trace. These digital touches are called "indicators" and are used by organizations to develop and organize their defensive intelligence. Generally, three types of indicators can be distinguished: atomic, computed, and behavioral.[a]

Atomic indicators are data that indicate possible offensive activities in their simplest form. Examples of atomic indicators include IP addresses, fully qualified domain names (FQDNs), email addresses, or a static string in a Command-and-Control (C2) channel. These indicators are the easiest to detect; however, using these to effectively build defensive capabilities can be problematic for an organization, as they may not always exclusively represent adversary activity. For example, an unknown program that triggers an antivirus solution can be malicious, but can also be a legitimate program which is not often used. Or, an IP address that is observed to be the IP from where an attack is launched could also belong to a legitimate site that was compromised. It is then that atomic indicators need additional investigation and correlation with other indicators or historical data to determine if they represent malicious activities performed by the guerilla band.

Computed indicators are (meta)data which form a representation of atomic indicators, usually captured in signatures. The most common computed indicators are the hashes of files: a small, unique representation of the file itself. The traditional antivirus mechanisms are based on computed hashes of files. Another example of this type of indicator is reputation-based values: based on multiple atomic indicators (eg, number of malicious files hosted, location and number of connections) the reputation value of an IP address can be computed (next-generation firewalls use these kinds of signatures).

Behavioral indicators are those which combine other indicators and observed behaviors to form a profile. For example, the guerilla band uses a compromised web server (with IP address 1.2.3.4 in country X) to serve malware to company Y's highly privileged administrators in country Z by sending them

---

[a]Source: "Security Intelligence: Attacking the Kill Chain" by Michael Cloppert (2009).

backdoored Microsoft Office documents, to establish C2 functionality with IP address 2.2.2.2 and gain persistent access to server A. The previous example contains a combination of atomic indicators (IP addresses 1.2.3.4 and 2.2.2.2, backdoored office documents), computed indicators (geolocation of IP addresses, hash values of the backdoored office documents, reputation of the website) and behavioral indicators (targets highly privileged administrators, creating persistent access to server A). Together, these indicators form a profile. In essence, the derived profiles aid cyber defense organizations to determine TTPs of hostile actors. However, since many (maybe indefinite) behaviors and indicators can be combined, it is hard to automatically generate a profile from behavioral indicators. Therefore intelligence-driven cyber security strongly depends on the capabilities of the targeted organization to determine the TTPs of their adversaries.

We will discuss cyber defensive strategies and corresponding TTPs to circumvent these in the following sections.

OPERATIONS

Multiple models exist to describe the operational life cycle of cyber attacks. Basically, most of them refer to some form of "kill chain": a set of generic steps or phases characterizing cyber attacks. The two most commonly used kill chains in the cyber defense industry are the "Cyber Kill Chain" and the "Advanced Persistent Threat" (APT) life cycle. Whereas the former kill chain specifically focuses on the steps required before actually entering a target's digital boundaries (or network), the APT life cycle focuses on the actions required once initial access has been obtained. Therefore, they partially overlap and complement each other. This section will discuss these two models as they are essential for understanding how operations are planned and performed. Understand that the time it takes to complete specific steps in the cyber kill chain may be disproportionate to each other. For example, the first six steps of the Cyber Kill Chain can sometimes be performed in days, while the last step ("complete actions on objectives") can take weeks or months. To deal with this disproportionality, we will substitute the last three steps after the "exploitation phase" of the cyber kill chain by the phases of the APT life cycle.

Furthermore, the cyber kill chain solely relates to intrusion by malware, which only covers a small subset of possible attack vectors that the guerilla band can use. For example, why would you try to infect a legitimate user with malware if you could either steal the target's data by exploiting an SQL injection in a publicly accessible web application or have an insider steal the data for you? We will therefore enrich the cyber kill chain and also consider other attack vectors, such as remote access, exploiting vulnerabilities, insider threat, social engineering, and supply chain attacks.

Cyber kill chain

The "cyber kill chain"[b] consists of the following steps:

1. Reconnaissance: select targets and determine attack methods and preferred TTPs.
2. Weaponization: develop and test the attack methods.
3. Delivery: transmission of the attack via physical, email, web, or social engineering means.
4. Exploitation: successful initial penetration, access gained to target's infrastructure.
5. Installation: install malware, backdoors, and other software to gain remote control and persistent access.
6. Command-and-Control (C2): establish means to perform (remote) C2 throughout the target's infrastructure.
7. Actions on objectives: complete actions and achievements, cover tracks and digital traces.

The goal and strategy determine how the guerilla band performs the steps of the operational attack life cycle (see Chapter 1). Many TTPs can lead to the achievement of this goal, some more time-consuming or costly than others, but some also more easily detectable or invasive than others. It is up to the members of the guerilla band to determine which TTPs fit the goal best. However, the hacker group leadership should determine the boundaries in which their members can operate. Boundaries can be defined by financial investments (some operations are more costly), stealthiness, timeliness (some operations need to be completed before a specific deadline), required knowledge, required soft- and hardware, and number of resources. As described in Chapter 1, these considerations depend largely on the societal context, the state (training, skill, experience, etc.) of the hacker group, and that of the opponent.

An important aspect of cyber guerilla is that the used TTPs can change throughout all steps of the attack life cycle. It is therefore recommended, when performing the steps sequentially, to create a feedback loop back into the start of the kill chain (the "reconnaissance phase"). At any given moment, new information or events can change the effectiveness and efficiency of the chosen TTP, which requires the guerilla band to review their current

---

[b]Source: Lockheed Martin: http://cyber.lockheedmartin.com/intelligence-driven-defense-and-the-cyber-kill-chain

tactic and determine if it should be adapted or changed. In the end the goal of the mission should be achieved without compromising the boundaries set forth by the commander. If the new or adapted TTP supersedes one of these boundaries, permission must be asked before continuing.

For example, consider a guerilla band that has the goal to disrupt services provided by a public organization. Because the organization is highly dependent on a publicly available web service, the tactic of the guerilla band is to disrupt the main web application that supports this critical business process. The proposed TTPs should match this tactic and stay within the determined boundaries. If the guerilla band is unable to obtain detailed information on their target during the reconnaissance phase, they may decide to choose a more generic TTP, such as infecting the PC of the main administrator and misusing his privileged access to disrupt the web service or performing a denial-of-service attack directly on the targeted web service. Both TTPs, infecting the PC of the main administrator or launching a denial-of-service attack, have their (dis)advantages and each has different characteristics in terms of financial investment, effectiveness, stealth, and timeliness. During the execution of the specific TTP, the guerilla band might identify relevant pieces of information that can change their attack vector and TTPs. For example, if it turns out that the identified web service is running on a very outdated or insecurely configured middleware layer (eg, Java, PHP, or ASP), it can become more beneficial or efficient to change attack vector and exploit the identified weaknesses in the middleware directly. Therefore, it is not required that the guerilla band completes all steps of the kill chain, or executes them sequentially.

Reconnaissance

In the reconnaissance phase the guerilla band determines the easiest or most effective way to achieve the determined goal, following the strategy and boundaries set forth by the leadership. To determine the most effective and/or efficient TTPs, multiple scenarios should be developed. Apart from determining the "most beneficial," "most likely," and "worst case" scenarios, it is of utmost importance to gather correct, relevant, and timely information on multiple aspects of the target. We will discuss the most common here, which can be divided into organizational, procedural, and technical aspects. Insights into these aspects help determine what means should be developed (or bought) and what type of TTP is feasible, given the circumstances.

Organizational aspects

Information on the organizational aspects not only provides the guerilla band with the weakest spots of their target, but also aids to determine the follow-up and possible response procedures that are followed by the entity in the case the hacker group's activities are detected. We would recommend to at least gather some information on the following aspects:

- Cultural aspects. The way individuals or affiliates of the target entity are treated. This includes the level of awareness on possible cyber intrusions. Important when the hacker group requires insider help or employs bribing.
- Organizational structure. The different units, departments, and key figures.
- Languages used. Especially important when social engineering is employed.
- Financial information. The budgets, costs, and turnover. For example, the average or specific income of employees can help determine if employees can be bribed. Also, the IT and security budgets can tell something about the level of defense of the target organization.
- Geographical spread. The different (physical) locations of the entity.
- Critical processes. The most critical business processes the target entity relies on. Especially important if the hacker group is planning sabotage.
- Online presence. The organization's communication channels such as (corporate) websites, presence on social media, and connections with traditional media (radio/television). Also includes preferred communication channels of the individuals related to the entity, such as employees and suppliers.
- Offline presence. When the hacker group decides to physically interfere with the target entity or its representatives, it should also consider the physical security of the entity. This could include guards, motion sensors, location and type of cameras, reception employees, fences, and terrain. If the strategy of the group is to target key individuals of an entity, such as members of the board and their secretaries, main IT administrators, or guards, the hacker group should also consider gathering information on (private) addresses, hobbies, and habits of these key personnel.

This information helps the hacker group to better determine their goal, strategy, and corresponding TTPs. For example, it is less feasible to launch a distributed denial-of-service attack on a target that has a large geographical spread (multiple data centers) than a target that only sits in few locations. Another example is the correct usage of language and context, especially for launching attacks that require human interaction. Effective phishing is much easier when the native language of the targeted organization is used in the campaign.

Defensive processes and mechanisms

The hacker group should determine how adequate the protection and defense mechanisms are at the target entity. For example: what kind of firewalls do they have? Is a cyber defense or information risk management function present? What is their level of monitoring and response? Do they have a media strategy? Have they been hacked before, and what was their response?

A good way to find information on the defensive processes and mechanisms is "fingerprinting," which can be done passively and actively. Passive fingerprinting entails the process of using all kinds of sources to gather information, but without actively interfering with these sources. Although passive fingerprinting is stealthy and not easily detected, is does not always provide enough information.

Active fingerprinting is the process of actively interacting with the target entity, either by using social means, such as calling or emailing, or technical means, such as scanning. For example, the guerilla band can decide to actively infiltrate social media groups and obtain knowledge on interpersonal connections that indicate presence of specific hard- and software. For example, if an employee of the targeted organization has many connections with employees of a firewall vendor, chances are high they also use that firewall brand.

Another important aspect of active fingerprinting is to determine how adequate and effective the defensive processes in the targeted organization are. For example, the guerilla band could develop and send their target general looking malware. Although this malware should definitely not reveal the intentions and goal of the hacker group, it can be programmed to gather as much information as possible. Although the malware might be easily detected by the entity; it can also bring valuable information on the target infrastructure and it can show the guerilla band how quickly the malware is detected, how easy it was for the organization to respond, and if the user(s) are aware. Futhermore, this piece of malware can provide all kinds of technical information, such as operating systems used, applications installed and the type of network segregation implemented. This is crucial information to perform a more sophisticated attack later in the campaign.

Technical aspects—available infrastructure and architecture

A good starting point for gathering information is the extranet. The extranet is defined as all web and communication services publicly accessible over the Internet. If the strategy of the guerilla band is to compromise systems, disrupt processes, or steal data available in the extranet, they should determine which services and systems are present. This reconnaissance activity aids in determining if vulnerabilities in the extranet are present which can be exploited to achieve the guerilla's goal. Depending on the goal and strategy, the guerilla band can use the following "layers" of the Open Systems Interconnection model (OSI)[c] as a guide:

Infrastructure layer

- Determine which systems, hostnames, and entities belong to the target entity. More specifically, find out which IP ranges, DNSs, FQDNs, Autonomous System Numbers (ASN), and registrars are used.
- Determine which services and their corresponding software versions are running on the identified infrastructure. A common way to identify these services is to use port scanning tools.
- If physically near, determine which wireless protocols and authentication mechanisms are used.

Application layer

- Determine which application server (middleware such as Java, Tomcat, JBoss, or IBM Websphere), application programming interface, and additional code framework versions are used.
- Determine which web servers (such as Apache, Nginx, or IIS) are available, and which versions are running.
- Determine if database systems can be reached over the Internet, and if so, which versions are running.
- Determine the level of filtering and remote accessibility: can any sensitive information be reached? A common attack method is the so-called "forceful browsing": the guerilla band tries to guess or in other ways construct a hidden URL to obtain access to sensitive information directly.
- Determine if injection possibilities are present. An injection attack can be executed on multiple layers of the target infrastructure. The most common form can be executed by injecting database commands into a web application that does not filter user input correctly—a so-called "SQL injection," which often provides unauthorized direct access to data in the database. Other forms of injection can be found if misconfiguration or coding errors exist in the interpreting layer (middleware such as ASP, PHP, or JSP) or by misusing insecure upload functionality that allows the hacker group to upload malicious files and code.
- Identify weak or broken authentication or session management. Is it possible to reach functionality which should have been protected by an authentication mechanism? Another common error made by many organizations is the usage of weak session identifiers

---

[c]Source: http://standards.iso.org/ittf/PubliclyAvailableStandards/index.html

(which authenticate the requests of legitimate users). If not enough randomness is used in the generation of the session identifier, the hacker group can guess the identifier of a legitimate user and obtain access to the protected part of the website.

■ Identify any miscellaneous security misconfigurations which can be exploited. Examples can be guessable passwords or default administrative interfaces.

Additional reconnaissance actions. Apart from the aforementioned layers, the hacker group should also perform reconnaissance of regular remote access methods that can be used by employees or members of the target entity to access their data and (internal) systems remotely. This includes access methods such as Virtual Private Network (VPN) and remote terminal services such as Citrix's Desktop As A Services (DAAS), the Microsoft Remote Desktop Protocol (RDP), and Secure Shell (SSH) on Unix-based systems.

It is also recommended to determine what the target architecture and infrastructure look like, for example, what level of network segregation is used. This can be performed actively, by launching network and port scans, or passively, by querying public information repositories for domain names, IP blocks, and autonomous systems. Sometimes unsuspecting employees or IT administrators of an organization post useful information on network architecture and system versions online by requesting help on a publicly accessible web forum.

Weaponization

In this phase the guerilla band maps the information, such as identified vulnerabilities and possible infiltration paths, to attack strategies and corresponding TTPs. The hacker group determines the most likely and most beneficial attack paths and starts preparation for the actual execution. Depending on the attack strategy, they can build malware, create an exploit, develop tools, derive word lists for password-cracking purposes, prepare phishing attacks, setup C2 structures, etc.

It is important to understand the difference between autonomic attacks and human-supported attacks. An autonomic attack can be described as "fire and forget": it requires a large preparation effort, but when it is directed at the entity it will go through the phases in the attack life cycle automatically without interaction of the hacker group. The Stuxnet malware is an example of an autonomic attack; it used different preprogrammed exploit and delivery methods, thereby propagating through targeted networks automatically and sabotaging the goal systems without interference of the attacker. The hacker group should not unnecessarily aim to use autonomic attacks, as the costs in time and manpower will most likely be higher than the benefits. It requires a very high skill level, detailed information about the target (such as version information of internal systems), and a large preparation effort. Also, the developed malware should be completely foolproof and should be able to anticipate all scenarios. As the guerilla band will often find themselves with incomplete information about their target, they cannot easily build such malware and therefore should not focus on creating autonomic attacks, but rather focus on human-supported attacks. Effectiveness should always prevail above technical perfection or beauty.

In a human-supported attack, the guerilla band performs all the steps of the operational life cycle manually (although they still can automate some of the activities). This provides them with far more flexibility, such as changing a TTP during the campaign, and requires less preparation effort than autonomic attacks. A human-supported attack also requires less information to execute. Additional information and data for executing the next steps in the kill chain can be collected and used to create new attack vectors on the go.

Another important aspect in the weaponization phase is the distinction between direct and indirect delivery. With a direct delivery, the guerilla band uses methods that do not require human interaction with the targeted entity, for example, by launching a SQL-injection attack on the web application or exploiting an unpatched firewall vulnerability. Indirect delivery requires the hacker group to interact with humans related to the targeted entity, for example, by sending employees a phishing mail with malware or bribing a corrupt affiliate.

We list the most common attack mechanisms per type of delivery:

- Direct delivery (does not require human interaction)
  - Exploitation of uncommon vulnerabilities (zero days)
  - Exploitation of common vulnerabilities
    - Exploit vulnerable software
    - Guessing weak passwords
    - Injection attacks
    - Misusing configuration issues
  - Physical delivery
  - Denial-of-service (DOS)
- Indirect delivery (requires human interaction)
  - (Spear)phishing
  - Watering hole
  - Supply chain
  - Insider help

The attacks listed are nonexclusive: if required or allowed within the boundaries set forth by the leadership, direct and indirect attack vectors can be used concurrently in the same campaign. In the next section we will describe how these attack methods can be executed to gain the successful initial penetration and the first access to the target's infrastructure.

Delivery

Many of the attack methods developed in the weaponization phase require a specific type of delivery. We will consider direct versus indirect delivery mechanisms and discuss per attack mechanism how it can be applied based on the information gathered during the reconnaissance and weaponization phases.

Direct delivery

Exploitation of common vulnerabilities. The easiest delivery method is the exploitation of common security vulnerabilities, such as guessing passwords, misusing configuration issues, injection attacks, and exploiting software with known security issues. The possibilities for the hacker group are endless, as organizations are usually unable to completely protect their systems. The larger the organization, the larger the surface of applications and infrastructure that can be reached over the Internet and thereby the higher the probability of security vulnerabilities that can be exploited. If the target data are stored on systems reachable over the Internet (such as web applications that provide access to a database) or the guerilla band's strategy does not require compromising internal systems (such as performing a DOS or website defacement attack), it might suffice to find a common vulnerability to exploit.

Depending on the strategy and TTP, they can choose to look for common vulnerabilities breadth-first or depth-first. The breadth-first search strategy is used when the target data or system are not yet identified and the hacker group just needs access to any machine or application. After exploiting common issues on this system, they can try and escalate their access to other systems, for example, with the information found on the initially compromised system. To efficiently identify common vulnerabilities, they can use automated techniques such as scanning tools. They should be aware that these automatic techniques can stand out in network traffic analysis, which can reveal (the intentions of) the hacker group.

During the depth-first strategy, on the other hand, the guerilla band already knows which system or data they need to target (such as a publicly available database) and specifically look for common vulnerabilities to exploit in that system. Although this requires less automatic scanning to be performed, it is uncertain if the targeted system actually contains a security flaw.

Exploitation of uncommon vulnerabilities—zero day. A zero day is a previously undisclosed vulnerability for which no security patch is known to be available to date. As it requires expert knowledge to find and exploit zero days, they are often bought (eg, on a black market). Compared to governments or nation states, digital guerilla operations tend to be low cost. If members of the guerilla band do not have the specific knowledge or financial assets in their team to create or buy a zero day that matches their target's infrastructure.

They are bound to less costly means to perform the initial compromise. Although a zero day is a very effective way to obtain an initial compromise in the target's network, it requires special skills to develop or is very costly to buy. Furthermore, it has to be developed exactly for the target's infrastructure and software used. Commonly, this is knowledge which is not available to the guerilla at the start of their campaign.

Physical delivery. When a member of the guerilla band is in the proximity of the target entity's physical premises, the hacker group can decide to deliver the attack physically. For example, by trespassing the physical boundaries, sending malicious files on USB sticks, installing remote access hard- and software, or breaking into the wireless network, the hacker group can obtain unauthorized access to the (internal) network and systems of the entity. Although this type of delivery has a high probability of success, the members executing the attack are more exposed to the risk of identification and detection than when the attack delivered is purely digital. For example, when performing a social engineering attack on the reception personnel of the target entity in order to gain physical access to the network ports of the internal network, the member of the hacker group executing the attack cannot easily hide his identity and is unable to escape the moment he is caught in action. Therefore it requires a specific type of personality to perform these kinds of attacks. This guerilla member should not easily panic, be able to perform physical social engineering, excel in disguise, and preferably should blend in with the culture of the targeted entity.

Denial-of-service (DOS). Where the other direct delivery methods focus on obtaining access to systems and data, a DOS attack focuses on sabotage. We can distinguish multiple levels of a DOS:

- Performing a DOS attack by sending so much data or packets to a (network) service such that it cannot handle the volume anymore, also called a Distributed Denial-Of-Service (DDOS). If desired, some form of amplification can be used, by using the DNS protocol or the Network Time Protocol (NTP).

■ Performing a DOS attack by exploiting a (zero-day) vulnerability that explicitly (irrecoverably) damages the target system.

■ Performing a DOS attack by infiltrating into the network and corrupting or erasing data and systems on purpose. A major example of such an attack is the Shamoon virus that erased 30,000 systems of the oil company Saudi Aramco in 2012.

Sabotage and DOS targeted at systems is less effective as sabotage targeted at (parts of) the IT or business operations chain. This is due to the so-called "multiplier" effect: errors or faults in the first elements of the chain will cause more damage later, especially if multiple stages in the chain are targeted at the same time. For example, consider a hacker group that is able to break into a financial institution, such as an insurance company, and wants to perform sabotage. By inserting faults in the initial stages of the insurance registration process, it will be more costly for the targeted institution to deal with corrupt data later in the process than to simply restore the (single) system that was sabotaged otherwise.

Indirect delivery
Spear-phishing attacks. A proven way of success is social engineering via spear phishing: a low-cost and effective way to perform initial penetration and establish a foothold in a target's network. However, performing a social engineering attack that leads to the right initial compromise requires planning and extensive information about the target. Spear fishing is a special form of regular phishing, directed at specific individuals in the targeted organization. It requires the attacker to gather specific and personal information about their target to increase the probability of success. This information is then used to craft a scenario that increases the level of trust between the attackers and the target.

A good example of performing an initial compromise via spear fishing is sending exploit code to the target via email or tricking him into opening a URL or malicious program. Java applets and Microsoft's Office macros are low-cost and effective ways to perform this kind of exploitation. The guerilla band should start their campaign by gathering as much information as possible to profile the target. For instance, if high-privileged individuals have been identified, the guerilla band focuses on gathering personal information about these targets. With this information a scenario should be defined to determine at what moment and how the exploit code is transferred to the target.

To gain a higher a level of trust, it is not recommended to immediately send malware to the target. The target first needs to get acquainted and the attackers should establish some trustworthiness. It is effective to set up communications with the targets in multiple ways, for example, via email and telephone. Once the guerilla band is confident that the target will open the malicious document or link, the exploit code should be hidden inside a normal document (that matches the chosen scenario). For example, if a Windows Office macro is used, it is recommended to wrap the exploit code in an inconspicuous-looking document. If Java is used, it is recommended to obtain a valid code signing certificate. This will reduce the number of warnings to launch the malicious code and will help to maintain the required level of trust with the target. Providers of (code signing) certificates, the so-called "Certificate Authorities," often have holes in their identity verification and certificate request processes which can be misused by a hacker group to obtain a valid certificate under a false identity.

The guerilla band should ensure that the exploit code matches the target's software environment. For example, a Microsoft Office macro will not launch on a Unix device and a Java applet will not execute if Java is not present on the target system. To obtain this information, it is recommended that a fingerprint attack is launched early in the execution of the campaign. This can be as simple as having the target visit a specifically crafted website that fingerprints the browser, user agent, software used, operating system version, and possible browser extensions. There are freely available tools online that can aid in this process.[d] With the obtained information, a new, more trustworthy, and up-to-date scenario can be created, or the current scenario can be adapted. Another advantage of establishing multiple ways of communications and interaction with the individual targets is to determine if they are willing to take the bait. A target that is already skeptical in the initial communication moments is less likely to get compromised than a target that turns out to be willing to, unwittingly, aid the guerilla band in achieving the initial compromise.

Another important aspect of the spear-phishing technique is to ensure that the communication loop is closed. If the communication with a target consists of multiple stages, for example, multiple email messages or phone calls, it is recommended to properly finish the communication with the target. This could be as simple as sending a message asking if the delivered services were up to standard or if the attachment could be opened without any problems. Closing the communication loop decreases the chance that the target becomes suspicious after the exploit code has been opened and provides the guerilla band with another communication opportunity in case the exploit failed or ceased to operate.

---

[d]For example: www.browserleaks.com

Although there are many ways to perform spear phishing, they all depend on the willingness of the targeted individuals to perform an action which is beneficial for the attacker. To improve the chance of success, the following forms of persuasion can be used to increase influence on a target[e]:

1. Reciprocity. The guerilla band should create a scenario in which their victim tends to return them a favor, for example, by providing their victim with free "software."
2. Commitment and consistency. The hacker group should ensure that their victims honor their commitment by expressing it explicitly (either orally or in writing), such that they establish the goal as being congruent with their self-image.
3. Social proof. Humans tend to do things they see or hear other humans doing. The guerilla band can use this to their advantage to create a scenario in which they have their victim open a malicious document by stating that his colleagues also opened it. In this example, it will be more trustworthy if the hacker group has determined the names and contact details of colleagues.
4. Authority. If the hacker group impersonates authoritative individuals, such as a CEO or a police officer, the victims of the hacker group are more likely to perform an action as they tend to obey authority.
5. Liking. If the guerilla band is well prepared and invests time in getting to know their victim, they can try to create a bond. If their victim likes the member of the hacker group, he can be more easily persuaded to perform an action.
6. Scarcity. The hacker group can use the argument of scarcity to create a feeling of urgency with their target.

Watering hole attacks. Instead of directly targeting its victim, the guerilla band can also use other forms of delivering the exploit code to the target, such as the so-called "watering hole attack." During a watering hole campaign, a strategic web or Internet facing server is compromised and used to serve malware to its visitors. This campaign is aimed at infecting the cyber guerillas' true target. The hacker group has no real interest in the owner of the infected server other than using it to continue the real attack. Depending on the goal and strategy of the guerilla band, these opportunistically compromised (web) servers can also be used to launch DOS attacks or serve malware, or be repurposed as a phishing site. If the website is used to serve malware or as a phishing site, it is important that the real targets frequently visit this site. Therefore, it should be strategically chosen to increase probability of a successful infection. For example, in 2015 the Hacking Team

---

[e]Source: "Influence: Science and Practice" by Robert Cialdini (2009).

leaks revealed that employees of Hacking Team compromised websites that were typically visited by organizations from a particular target or competing industries, thereby maximizing the effectiveness of the watering hole attack. On one occasion, the group was associated with tracking the movement of suspected activists of the group Mamfakinch online by publishing a document supposedly containing compromising information about a Moroccan politician. Instead, the document contained tracking malware.

The guerilla band should consider a strategy to lure their victims to an infected website by publishing interesting information about, or in the interest of, the targeted organization.

Supply chain attacks. Many entities and organizations are dependent on all kinds of IT-related hard- and software suppliers. These suppliers have some form of access to the environment of the targeted entity, either to perform maintenance or to install new hard- or software, which together form the so-called "delivery chain". Once the guerilla band determines which suppliers have access to their target, the hacker group should develop a TTP that corresponds to usage of the parties in the delivery chain. Although this strategy requires more reconnaissance effort and intelligence, it could be highly effective as the target entity usually has a high level of trust with its vendors and suppliers. For example, during the largest digital heist in 2013, hackers broke into the core systems of the Bank of Oman by infecting systems of its Indonesian IT supplier.

We will discuss applications of supply chains attacks later, when dealing with attacks on segregated networks.

Insider help. A very effective delivery method is using insider help. For example, employees who have high-privileged access to data, who are willing to smuggle a virus on a USB stick, or knowingly download malware, can easily provide the guerilla band with the required access to data and systems.

The most time-consuming but important part of this type of delivery method is to identify the people who are willing to cooperate. Although threats and blackmail are very effective methods to gain insider cooperation, these methods will also have a (negative) impact on the reputation of the hacker group and their cause. It would be better to identify individuals who are willing to voluntarily aid the hacker group and its cause. The guerilla band should find out what the possible motives are for insiders to help. For example, can they identify themselves with the cause of the hacker group or are they just disgruntled?

If the guerilla band has sufficient financial assets, they might also want to consider paying insiders to deliver the attack, or smuggle the required data out.

Exploitation, installation, command and control and actions on objectives

The previously described Cyber Kill Chain is a decent model to describe the operational life cycle of a digital guerilla attack. However, it does not provide the attacker with a detailed description of the steps taken after the initial compromise and specifically focuses on completing the attacker's goal by launching malware against a target. Although for some goals and attack strategies the "initial compromise" might suffice, many more advanced scenarios and TTPs require deeper penetration into a target's network and systems. We will therefore substitute the last four steps of the cyber kill chain, "Exploitation," "Installation," "Command and Control," and "Actions on Objectives," with the advanced persistent threat life cycle.

Advanced persistent threat life cycle

The APT life cycle[f] focuses on the phases after the initial compromise (or "exploitation" phase). Similar to the cyber kill chain, it also comprises seven steps:

1. Initial compromise
2. Establish foothold
3. Escalate privileges
4. Internal reconnaissance
5. Move laterally
6. Maintain presence
7. Complete mission

These steps will be discussed in the following sections. As discussed before, note that depending on the attack strategy and tactics, not all steps have to be completed or executed sequentially and can also be done in parallel. In Fig. 3.1 these steps are depicted with a dotted rectangle. Furthermore, steps 3 through 6 can be executed iteratively to increase the scope of systems that can be controlled by the guerilla band.

Initial compromise

The initial compromise, the system on which some form of access is obtained first, is performed by using any of the methods described earlier, such as social engineering and spear phishing, over email, using zero-day exploits, or direct attacks. In the "initial compromise" phase, the guerilla band actually executes the prepared attack path and gains access to a system or premise of the target. It is important to compromise a system which is

---

[f]Source: Mandiant http://intelreport.mandiant.com/

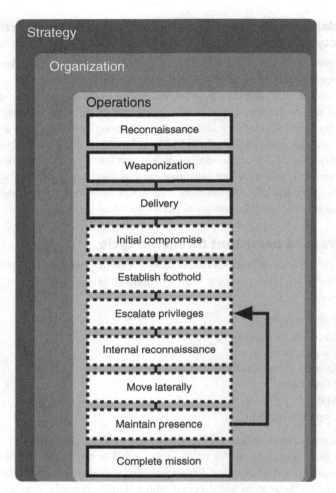

■ **FIGURE 3.1 Operational life cycle of offensive cyber operations.**

strategically positioned in the targeted entity. This does not necessarily have to be a system that is operated by an individual with high privileges in the targeted network. For example, if the guerilla band discovers during the reconnaissance phase that the target data are stored in a mailbox of a specific employee, it might not even be required to compromise a single system. Depending on the configuration of the targeted organization's email structure, it might well suffice to obtain access to the webmail box of this specific employee by retrieving his credentials for the webmail service.

Also, if the goal of the guerilla campaign is to sabotage the targeted organization, and the organization is highly dependent on its industrial control systems (systems that control the physical processes of a production chain, often physically segmented from the general office network), it might be more successful for the attackers to compromise a system close to or in the industrial control network. This possibly requires a different approach, for example by infecting an engineering support company in the supply chain rather than targeting the organization or its employees directly. We will discuss dealing with segregated networks later.

Establish foothold

After the initial compromise is executed, the guerilla band should plant remote administration software in the targeted network, create (network) backdoors and (reverse) tunnels to allow for remote C2 and covert access to the target infrastructure. It is important to use multiple channels to ensure that the cyber attack can continue if one or more access points are detected or closed. This also means the hacker group should make their remote administration software persistent, thereby ensuring that their malware survives a reboot, or even reinstall, of the targeted machine. We will later describe techniques for obtaining persistence and keeping the C2 structures undetected.

Escalate privileges

Depending on the goal, strategy, and chosen TTPs, the guerilla band can find themselves in the position where they have limited access rights on the device (server, laptop, etc.) after first compromise. For example, if the hacker group successfully exploited a vulnerability in the web server software they have the access rights of that software on the underlying operating system. If they have infected a regular employee (eg, through spear phishing), they have the access rights of the employee on his workstation. As this is not always a sufficient form of access, the hacker group can perform so-called "vertical privilege escalation": upgrading the access rights from the current user or process to the user or process with higher access rights on the compromised machine (such as an administrator). By doing so, the guerilla band can retrieve important system files (such as the file where the passwords of other users are stored), create backdoors more easily, and possibly login to other systems and services (so-called "lateral movement," which will be described later).

Common vertical privilege escalation paths are as follows:

- Searching for passwords of higher privileged accounts that are stored in (configuration) files on the compromised machine.
- Editing scripts or (service) executables that are launched with high privileges (eg, during boot time).
- Editing the source code of a web application that is running with high privileges.

- Exploiting a common or zero-day vulnerability in the operating system or web application that is running with high privileges.
- Misuse configuration errors, such as unquoted service paths in Windows.

It is important to understand that vertical privilege escalation is optional. As discussed earlier, the guerilla band should not perform privilege escalation if it does not serve a purpose or when it is just used to show off to others. For many TTPs it is sufficient to have a compromised machine that just provides network-level access to the target network, without requiring high privileges on that specific machine.

Internal reconnaissance

When the guerilla band has successfully established a foothold and infected one or more systems in the internal network of the target entity, it can start collecting new information as the obtained network position provides a new perspective on data and systems in the internal network. The process for internal reconnaissance is the same as the initial reconnaissance step in the cyber kill chain. However, more detailed information can be gathered in the internal network, which can also be used for performing privilege escalation and lateral movement later. Depending on the required goal and TTPs, the following additional information can be collected:

- If a Windows Active Directory structure is implemented, the hacker group can use the access credentials of the user or system obtained during the initial compromise to query the domain controllers, central systems that are used for authentication, for detailed information. Information such as (privileged) user groups, password complexity requirements, access rights, open network shares, trust relationships with other domains, and the application portfolio can be determined.
- Semiopen data repositories and unstructured data sources such as file shares (SMB or NFS), Windows Sharepoint, and proprietary data collections can be enumerated and searched. These data repositories are often underestimated as source of information. On many occasions we noted that these sources contain plain text passwords, configuration files, (web) application source code, confidential information, application manuals, backups, business process descriptions, and internal communication messages or even email archives.
- The hacker group can perform internal network scanning to determine the level of network segregation, network architecture, and identify vulnerable services. However, launching large-scale network scanning should be avoided because it can easily be detected and can disturb or even destroy the C2 channel to the compromised machine.

- Determine the security monitoring maturity of the targeted entity. We will discuss tactics to deal with the different levels of security monitoring later.
- Determine the access paths to the target systems and data. What other systems need to be compromised? Which accounts should be impersonated? In which database are the data stored?

Move laterally

In this phase the guerilla band tries to expand their control over other workstations, servers, and infrastructure devices. Contrary to vertical privilege escalation, lateral movement is a form of horizontal privilege escalation.

There are two different types of lateral movement, both of which have their own escalation process:

1. Increase the span of control from the initial compromised machine directly to the target system(s) and, if required, escalate privileges on the target system vertically.
2. Increase the span of control from the initial compromised machine to other (not specifically the target) systems first until sufficient access rights to gain access to the target system(s) are obtained. For example, in a Windows Active Directory environment, you want to obtain access to the highly privileged accounts that can login to the target system or retrieve the data you are after. Although it is not required to obtain the highest privileges within the Active Directory structure (the "Enterprise" or "Domain" administrator accounts), it can be very effective as it allows you to control all systems, users, and access rights connected to the domain. In large organizations, this means you can access more than 100,000 systems, including those of the members of the board. However, these accounts with the highest privileges are often better monitored for suspicious behavior.

Both the external and internal reconnaissance processes determine how long it takes to obtain access to the target system(s) or data. In large IT environments, we have seen examples that becoming domain administrator only took hours or days, while finding and compromising the final target systems took weeks or months. Apparently, it is not always easy to find what you are looking for immediately.

The disadvantage of the first escalation process is that as an attacker you either need a zero-day exploit or find a common vulnerability on the target system, which can be a time-consuming process. The advantage of this method is that it leaves a relatively small network footprint, which decreases the risk of detection.

The second escalation process has the advantage that it has a high probability of success because high-privileged accounts can provide access to nearly all systems and data. The disadvantage is that the process can be lengthy and leave a large footprint, which increases the risk of detection.

We describe the most common lateral movement paths:

- Spear phishing on highly privileged individuals within the targeted entity. For example, by sending them malicious documents directly, or luring them to a place in the internal network where they have to authenticate against a system under control by the hacker group. The moment the victim logs in to this system, credential stealing techniques can be applied to impersonate the victim or obtain access to his password. In many Windows systems connected via Active Directory, the hacker group can, when they have administrative access to the compromised machine, retrieve the so-called "Kerberos ticket" of the victim that logs in. Depending on the validity of the Kerberos ticket and the access rights of the victim within the Active Directory domain, the hacker group can replay that ticket to another machine and gain access to the resources as that user. This is commonly referred to as "pass-the-ticket" attack and is allowed in almost all versions of Windows.
- Many entities use the same passwords or authentication credentials (such as SSH keys on Unix) on multiple, or all, systems. In a Windows environment, it is often observed that the local administrator account is equal for all workstations and servers. If the guerilla band detects that this is the case, they first need to perform a local vertical privilege escalation attack to obtain access to the password hash of this local administrator account. They can then proceed to crack this hash and try to retrieve the password or use the password hash itself to authenticate to other systems, which is commonly referred to as "pass-the-hash" attack and is allowed in almost all versions of Windows. Because the password (and thus the corresponding password hash) is equal on all systems, the hacker group can easily perform lateral movement.
- In some entities the passwords of highly privileged accounts are stored on semiopen data repositories and unstructured data sources such as file shares, especially in configuration files and startup scripts located in the so-called "NETLOGON" share of the Windows domain controller systems.
- In a Windows Active Directory environment, the hacker group can try to find vulnerabilities in the domain controller systems, which provide access to highly privileged accounts directly.
- In a Windows Active Directory environment, the guerilla band can try to exploit vulnerabilities in any (Windows) system connected to the domain. When they succeed and obtain privileged access to a specific

machine, they can use the previously described credential stealing techniques to retrieve the plain text passwords of other logged in users from the memory (via the so-called "Local Security Authority Subsystem Service," LSASS), retrieve the previously described Kerberos ticket, or retrieve the password hashes of local users from disk (via the so-called "Security Account Manager," SAM, file). This works especially well on terminal servers and steppingstone systems, as these are used by many users and administrators to login. When they have obtained the credentials, the guerilla band can then use these to login to other systems and repeat this credential stealing process until they either have access to the target system or have the highest privileges within the domain (which also provides them access to the target system).

- In a Windows Active Directory environment, the hacker group can perform a reverse password brute force attack on the domain controller systems, which store the credential information of all users and systems in the corresponding Windows domain. During a reverse password brute force, the guerilla band does not iterate over the passwords, but iterates over the users: instead of trying multiple passwords for few users, the guerilla band should try a few, common, passwords for all users in the domain. Especially in large entities with many users, this has proven to be an effective tactic.
- In a Windows Active Directory environment, the hacker group can perform a so-called "man-in-the-middle attack" in which they actively inject network packets to influence the authentication protocols. Especially the so-called "SMB relay attack" and "WPAD responder attack" work well in practice. Both attacks misuse a configuration error in Windows to obtain access to password hashes and plain text passwords of legitimate users. Although these attacks can be very effective, it does require some form of interaction with the targeted users as they have to initiate the authentication protocol before the guerilla band can launch the attack.

Many more lateral movement tactics and techniques exist. To summarize, lateral movement is the art of escalating your privileges just as broad as you need to go deep.

Maintain presence

The guerilla band should ensure that they have continued control over their remote access channels and credentials obtained in the previous phases. Opposed to the active and synchronous call-back mechanisms for regular command and control (such as using regular protocols like HTTP and HTTPS), the guerilla band should also maintain one or more backup call-back mechanisms that are very asynchronous and cannot be correlated to the active C2 structure in case of a detection. This can be achieved by using common protocols that only leave a small network footprint, such as the DNS protocol or Internet Control Message Protocol (ICMP).

The guerilla band could also consider using call-back mechanisms that are hardly distinguishable from normal human behavior, such as visiting a common legitimate website and downloading a picture. This picture will contain the commands that the infected should execute, but they are encoded in such a way that only the infected machine will be able to read and execute these commands. This form of encoding is also called "steganography." For example, in 2015 the Hamertoss malware followed links in specific Twitter messages to obtain pictures stored on Github which contained the commands to execute. It would then upload the result of the executed commands to regular cloud storage services.

To use C2 mechanisms that are hardly distinguishable from normal human behavior, the guerilla band must gain information about regular user and protocol behavior in the targeted organization. It is also recommended to acquire knowledge on (cryptographic) steganography and message obfuscation techniques.

Apart from having continued control over their remote access channels, the guerilla band should ensure that they maintain access to the compromised systems when required (eg, through the authentication credentials, such as hashes and passwords, acquired during the campaign). Although it might be tempting to create new, highly privileged accounts (such as a Windows Enterprise or Domain Administrator account), adding or changing these types of accounts is often closely monitored. It is therefore recommended to impersonate regular (high-privileged) users and use their accounts to perform offensive actions. In a Windows environment (or a Linux environment that is connected to the Active Directory), this means that the guerilla band should ensure that they have access to the passwords (or password hashes) of the Domain Administrator or other highly privileged accounts. The hacker group should preferably use service accounts, which are often less monitored and, since these are not used by humans, "irregular behavior" of these accounts, is often not timely detected. In a Linux environment, the guerilla band should ensure that they have access to the passwords or private keys of powerful accounts, preferably accounts with access to the "sudo" mechanism, to obtain the highest privileges, ie, "root" privileges, when required. An effective tactic is to add the public key equivalent of the obtained, or the guerilla's own, private key to the compromised systems (in the so-called "authorized_keys" file), to ensure access is maintained without interfering too much with the system.

When maintaining presence for a longer period of time, it is recommended to make the network footprint as small as possible, to minimize the chance of detection. This can already be achieved with one compromised machine (and maybe one backup backdoor) and the password of a high-privileged account which can login to multiple machines. Instead of infecting all machines, the guerilla band should use this account to install malware or perform lateral movement when required. When (temporarily) done with the offensive actions, the malware should be removed again and the system should be brought back into its initial state, leaving almost no traces. For example, in many Windows Active Directory environments the "krbtgt" account is not periodically reset, which means it can be used to create access tokens for every user associated with the domain. Even the password hash, rather than the password for this account itself, is sufficient to maintain presence without even having access to a domain administrator account directly. Although we have seen multiple backdoor mechanisms in practice (such as introducing new vulnerabilities on purpose or installing remote administration software on every compromised machine), it is best to use a mechanism that does not leave any (malicious) traces on the systems or the network.

If it is required to continuously have command and control mechanisms or remote administration toolkits installed on multiple machines, it is recommended to place the main C2 functionality that communicates with the attacker infrastructure on just a few machines. The hacker group should designate one or two compromised systems that perform communication with the attacker infrastructure, while the rest of the compromised machines in the internal network of the targeted entity only connect to these two machines to retrieve commands and post the output back to the guerilla band. In a Windows environment this can easily be achieved by using the file-sharing protocol (SMB) to perform internal command and control. This mechanism prevents possible monitoring solutions from detecting C2 traffic from multiple internal systems towards the attacker-controlled infrastructure on the Internet. The hacker group can also use peer-to-peer networks to set up their C2 channels, which makes detection even harder.

Complete mission

The final step of the operational life cycle is to complete the mission, that is, perform the actions on the target systems such as stealing information, performing transactions, initiating sabotage, and extracting data. However, in this phase only the technical part of the mission is completed. Depending on the desired effect, there might be other targets in the hacker group's campaign; this does not necessarily mean that the overall mission is completed. We will discuss the nontechnical accomplishment of the overall mission later.

The time required to complete the mission is often disproportional to the time required to perform the (initial) compromise and lateral movement phases. Especially finding the right information to retrieve and initiating transactions can be very time consuming.

Some entities employ a form of Data Leakage Prevention (DLP), that detects if (large volumes of) sensitive data are sent outside the entity's network premises. If the guerilla band detects that such mechanism is present, it is recommended to use a form of encryption to exfiltrate the acquired data. For example, the guerilla band can attach data to an encrypted email and send it to an email address it has access to. However, often the email channels are closely monitored by the DLP and it is therefore recommended to use other forms of data extraction, such as encrypting the data and then uploading them to a public data transfer service. These services are often not considered as malicious and therefore the DLP system will possibly allow this form of data exfiltration.

CONSIDERATIONS DURING OPERATIONS

In this section we will discuss how to deal with network segregation, monitoring mechanisms, and encryption as these concepts are relevant for any and all stages of the previously described kill chains.

Target architectures and network segregation

When referring to target architecture, we define "architecture" as the structural design of the information environment, including the physical IT components, such as switches, firewalls, servers, and end-user devices. An architecture can manifest itself in multiple ways. For guerilla operations, especially the "network architecture" is an important aspect. For the sake of simplicity, we distinguish the following types of network architectures:

1. No network segregation
2. Limited network segregation
3. Full network segregation

Network segregation is defined as controlling access between network segments. A common error in many organizations is that they perceive network *segmentation*, the act of splitting a computer network into subnetworks (or subnets), equal to network *segregation*. The difference is that dividing a network into segments does not necessarily increase security, as traffic from one network segment to the other might still be allowed. Segregation is defined as actively controlling access between two or more network segments. For example, in many organizations there is a segment for servers (such as email, application servers, and databases) and a segment for clients (such as laptops, desktops, and mobile devices). Although these machines are in different segments, client systems do usually have unrestricted access to all network resources on the server systems. If the network is segregated, then only the network resources that are required for legitimate business purposes are accessible by the clients.

As an attacker, it is important to draft a plan on how to deal with segregation as network-level access to target systems is required to launch a remote attack. The level of segregation also determines the escalation path within the targeted entity once initial access is obtained. For example, if the guerilla band requires data from a specific database and this database is not directly connected to the internal network of the entity, they should focus on obtaining access to a system such as a "jump server" that does provide network-level access to this database.

Attacking a network without segregation

An entity that does not have network segregation has multiple or all of its "internal" systems connected to the Internet. Although this does not necessarily mean that it can be immediately compromised—as the entity still might have their software properly patched or might have their resources protected with other measures—it does provide the guerilla band with a large attack surface. The attacker still needs to go through the regular planning and cyber kill chain processes, but the weaponization and delivery phase as well as the actual execution can be efficient, as the number of vulnerable network services increases linearly with the actual number of reachable network services.

However, entities without network segregation are rarely seen in the 21st century because most of the modern Internet Service Providers (ISPs) provide their customers (either business or consumer) with network equipment that also acts as a firewall and router. Even consumer modems have a firewall configured that segregates the home network from the Internet. Therefore, the guerilla band should take into account that most of their targets will have some form of segregation.

Attacking a network with limited segregation

The majority of the possible target entities that employ a form of segregation will do that by means of a demilitarized zone (DMZ), also referred to as "perimeter network." A DMZ is a subnetwork (either logical or physical) that contains the entity's services that need to be externally facing, that is, reachable over the Internet. Examples of these services are web applications, email, telephony, and file servers (such as FTP). The DMZ acts as an additional layer of security as only these externally facing systems are directly exposed to the Internet. More sensitive servers and systems in the so-called "intranet," or internal network, cannot be (directly) reached over the Internet. In theory the systems in the DMZ are also unable to access the intranet, which provides additional protection in case the DMZ is compromised. However, in practice many organizations need to have some form of network access from the DMZ to the internal network and therefore an attacker has many opportunities to jump from a compromised system in the DMZ to the internal network. For example, an Internet-facing web application, placed in the DMZ, that provides functionality to take out insurance should be able to insert or modify data in the customer database, which is usually located in the internal network. A hacker group that compromises the web application server can misuse the database connection credentials stored on this server to set up a connection to the database itself (via the web application server).

Entities that want additional protection on top of a DMZ divide the internal network in specific network segments and segregate these from each other. As previously explained, then only the network resources that are required for business purposes are accessible in and between these networks. Luckily for the guerilla band, many large organizations (such as multinationals) are unable to implement full network segregation as many of their employees require access to a large number of services, systems, and functionality. It is almost impossible to implement network-level access control for all these entities without interfering with business continuity. Typically these organizations rely on access control on a higher layer, for example, on the application layer. This means that the guerilla band, once initial access to the internal network is obtained, can freely roam the internal network(s) looking for insecurely configured operating systems, vulnerable applications, misconfigured (administrative) interface, and systems protected by weak passwords. For example, a single Enterprise Resource Planning (ERP) system such as SAP, the beating heart of many organizations that usually contains business critical data, has on average more than 100 open network ports, all of which can potentially provide the guerilla band an additional attack vector once they have obtained access to the same (internal) network.

Three main strategies can be followed to remotely attack a network with limited segregation (apart from the "physical" or "supply chain" attacks, which can almost always be executed).

The first strategy is a direct attack on the DMZ. Depending on the goals and TTPs, the guerilla band misuses (un)known vulnerabilities, injection, password guessing attacks, or other security misconfiguration-related attacks to compromise an initial system in the DMZ.

The second strategy is an indirect attack on end-user systems (such as laptops), which are usually connected to the internal network of the target entity. In this campaign, the guerilla band usez (spear)fishing or a watering hole attack to install malware on end-user systems. From here, they proceed with targeting other internal systems.

The third strategy is scanning the complete external network, that is, the systems reachable over the Internet (also called the "extranet") for mis-configurations in the external firewall. The goal is to find vulnerable systems that are positioned in the internal network of the entity but are also directly reachable over the Internet. Although this does not occur often, we have seen examples of third-party or supplier systems that required to be reachable over the Internet, for example, to provide remote support or to directly access data. These systems could easily be compromised; neither the entity itself nor the entity's supplier took responsibility for protecting the systems.

Attacking a heavily segregated network

A minority of the entities that the hacker group will encounter will have near full network segregation. This means that access between network segments—clusters of systems with the same function and/or clusters of systems with the same security level or user groups—is actively controlled. It is typically seen in smaller organizations, governments, and in the defense and aerospace industries. Apart from these entities, (almost) full network segregation is often observed in networks that form a very interesting target for the guerilla band: Operational Technology (OT). These types of networks consist of hardware and software that control and monitor changes in industrial processes through interaction with physical devices (such as pumps, valves, and meters). They are also often referred to as Industrial Control Systems (ICS) or Supervisory Control And Data Acquisition (SCADA) networks. The technological advancements in ICS have occurred rapidly, especially with the rise of the 24-hour economy, globalization, time-critical manufacturing processes, and just in time supply management. Sectors such as Oil & Gas, Power & Utilities, water treatment, chemicals manufacturing, and transportation have caused a tremendous boost in research and development to automate and digitalize industrial processes. Back in the old days, engineers had to read out analog meters covered in grease and oil to determine the pressure of an oil pipeline, whereas contemporary offshore drilling platforms can be controlled without human interaction or onsite presence. Based on market demand, quality of produced products, or even CO_2 emission values, the ERP system connected to the ICS network can automatically, and in real time, scale production up or down respectively.

As these type of systems control physical processes, the damage caused by a (digital) attack to the ICS network is not only financial but also physical.

Therefore, it forms one of the important targets for (asymmetric) digital warfare. A successful attack can cause major incidents, pollution, or even death. And, apart from the physical damage, many organizations have become dependent on the digital control processes, leaving them vulnerable for DOS attacks. Whereas Stuxnet probably is out of the capabilities of a common hacker group, the attack on the power grid of Ukraine is perfectly within range of the hacker group. Since Ukraine went dark on New Year's Eve 2016, ICS attacks went mainstream.

Although operational technology networks are typically heavily segregated from the organization's internal network or the Internet, it is still possible to penetrate them. But, the attack paths diverge from attacking an internal office network. We will discuss the three most viable attack paths and strategies to attack heavily segregated networks.

The first strategy goes via the internal (office) network of the targeted entity. Initial access is obtained by executing the same TTPs as for attacking a limited segregated network. From the initial compromise the guerilla band should focus on escalating their privileges to systems which are (partly) connected to the segregated network. It is recommended to determine the logical process flow of data as many systems in the ICS networks need to export their data to the office network, such as the meter readings and other production (system) information. Therefore, it is important to determine which systems and individuals within the organization, such as engineers and network administrators, have access to the ICS network. Social media or the internal employee catalog can be good sources to start with. Also, so-called "jump" or terminal servers that provide access to the ICS network for administrators are a good starting point. Another common type of system that provides interconnections to the OT networks are the so-called "historians." These systems gather and store the historical production data of the industrial processes and therefore need to maintain a connection to these OT networks.

However, on some occasions we have observed that even a compromise of the complete internal office network (eg, by compromising a Windows Active Directory domain administrator account) does not directly lead to a compromise of the OT networks. For example, these networks have their own Windows Active Directory domain or another form of authentication and access control. Two-factor authentication, such as a password in combination with a physical access token, is often required to gain access to the Industrial Control Network. However, in such scenarios it is still possible to compromise the ICS network by installing malware on the desktops of highly privileged administrators and use their connection to digitally tailgate into the segregated network.

The second strategy is launching an attack that requires physical presence near or onsite of the targeted entity. If the target is in the close proximity of the guerilla band's geographical location, it can be beneficial for the hacker group to launch a physical-oriented attack. The effort to gain physical access to heavily segregated networks is often smaller than to gain logical access to these networks by compromising the internal office network and trying to logically "jump" to the segregated network. For example, gaining physical access to ICSs of a water treatment facility by trespassing the physical fences and opening up a cabinet locker is way easier than trying to break into the water treatment facility logically, which might not even be connected to the Internet. Another way is to obtain physical access to the network ports of the heavily segregated network by means of social engineering. Members of the guerilla band use some form of disguise to mislead security guards or trespass other forms of physical access control. They could then plant a remote access device or install malware directly onto the segregated network.

The third strategy deals with indirect attacks via the delivery chain such as vendors, suppliers, and engineering companies. Although this strategy requires more reconnaissance effort and intelligence, it could be highly effective. The guerilla band should determine which suppliers, vendors, and engineering companies have access to the segregated network, either to perform maintenance or to install new hard- or software. Once this is determined, the hacker group should develop a TTP that corresponds to usage of the parties in the delivery chain. For example, to infect systems in an OT network in a utility company, the guerilla band can use a supply chain attack by determining which engineers from a third-party company maintain and update the OT systems. Usually, the so-called "ladder logic," (eg, the logic that determines when a valve or pump should open or close) is uploaded to an OT network via a laptop or USB device of the (maintenance) engineer. Once these engineers have been identified, their equipment can be infected (eg, through spear phishing) when their devices are connected to their own company network or the Internet. The guerilla band should configure their malware in such a way that the moment the engineers are back to perform maintenance in the OT network, the malware is activated and jumps onto the ICSs. Even if the engineers do not connect their own laptop or USB device to the OT network, an infection can still be done by creating a backdoor in the soft- or hardware of a supplier of OT systems, such as supplier of SCADA software. However, this attack vector requires specific knowledge of the functionality of the OT systems. Since these systems and protocols are often proprietary, this knowledge is sparse.

Until now we only have described how a guerilla band can obtain access to the segregated network. While penetrating such a network can be difficult, exfiltrating data or setting up C2 structures to the infected systems in these networks can be even more difficult. Apart from some misconfigurations we have observed in practice, these networks generally do not allow systems and users in the segregated network to connect to the Internet directly. Experience teaches us, depending on the goals of the guerilla band, that two strategies can be employed.

If the goal is to infiltrate and sabotage, standalone malware can be used. This type of malware does not require a connection to the Internet and, once deployed, it automatically searches relevant systems, infects them, and completes the actions on the target. However, as we have seen with the well-known "Stuxnet" virus, this requires major efforts in planning, preparation, intelligence, development, and manpower. Efforts a typical guerilla band might lack. Also, you need to know exactly what kind of systems, software, and connections are used to make your malware successful.

If the goal is to exfiltrate data or if the guerilla band cannot use standalone malware, it is often still possible to set up an active C2 structure and maintain persistence in heavily segregated networks. The most effective way is through "pivoting": using systems that can connect to two or more different networks simultaneously and routing the C2 traffic through these systems (the pivot points). Depending on the infrastructure and allowed protocols, pivot points can be set up in a chain. For example, we have observed that attackers were able to successfully set up a pivot chain to an ICS by misusing a mix of regular protocols and pivot points. The first step was to infect an administrator machine of the internal office network of the target by spear phishing. C2 with attacker-controlled systems could be performed via a regular Internet protocol, HTTPS. The administrator machine could set up a connection to the Historian server with the Windows file transfer protocol (SMB). Systems in the ICS network could connect to the Historian server (to upload production data), but (in this case) the Historian could not connect back. Through the pivot chain, the attacker placed an infected file on the file share on the Historian server that was downloaded and executed by the systems in the ICS network. Upon infection, the exfiltration of data and command and control of the industrial systems could be done by a somewhat surprising protocol: the DNS protocol. It turned out that the systems in the ICS network were not allowed to access the Internet directly, but were allowed to perform DNS requests to the internal DNS server, which in turn forwarded the requests to a DNS server on the Internet. By appending data to these DNS requests, the attacker could successfully set up a command and control channel to a DNS server he controlled. As the functionality of common protocols, such as DNS, is often overlooked in heavily segregated networks, it can be beneficial for the guerilla band to use these protocols for data exfiltration and command-an-control.

Dealing with monitoring and defense systems

In the past the most valuable data assets were more tangible and easily protected by putting them in a (digital) vault, for example, in structured sources such as databases. As a result of this tangibility and simplicity, companies had organized their IT security on a *system* level. This means that on a technical or operational level, the individual systems were usually reasonably well protected. With the increase of interconnected systems, organizations are becoming aware that they are continuously exposed to all kinds of digital threats. Since some companies get attacked even thousands of times a day, many of them have enhanced their detection capabilities and organized their IT security on a *data* level.

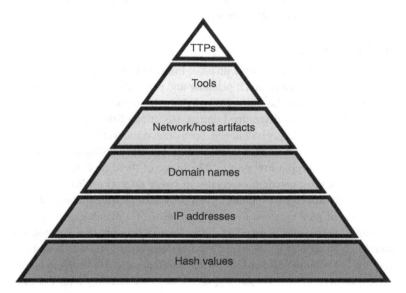

■ **FIGURE 3.2 The Pyramid of Pain.** The better an organization is able to detect the types of indicators at the top of the pyramid, the more pain it causes for attackers to change their offensive behaviors.

In the cyber defense industry, monitoring levels are typically modeled after the so-called "pyramid of pain" principle (Fig 3.2).[f] This model shows the relationship between the specific types of indicators the defensive teams might use to detect attackers' activities and how much pain they can inflict

---

[f]Source: "The Pyramid of Pain" by David Bianco (2013).

on the attackers when they are able to deny these indicators to them. Indicators can be, from bottom to top: hash values of malicious files (computed), IP addresses used by the attacker (atomic), domain names used by the attacker (atomic), network/host artifacts (computed and atomic), tools used by the attacker (behavioral), and TTPs (behavioral). The better the defensive organization is at detecting indicators at the top of the pyramid, the more pain it will inflict on the hacker group to change its behavior and stop generating these indicators to decrease the chance of detection again. We will use the pyramid of pain model to define the maturity levels of monitoring an organization might have:

1. No monitoring/ad hoc detection and responsive measures. Focuses on the lower part of the pyramid.
2. Limited monitoring (eg, network-based or host-based only). Focuses on the middle part of the pyramid.
3. Extensive monitoring and follow-up (eg, asset-based/data-centric). Focuses on the top part of the pyramid.

Ad hoc detection

Obviously, attacking an entity with no or limited monitoring is not very difficult. It does not require much planning and preparation other than finding the right target within the entity and launching the initial compromise attack. Specific TTPs can be determined during execution of the campaign. Once initial access to the target is obtained, open-source and well-known scanning and hacking tools can be used to achieve the guerilla's goals, as it is simply not required to keep a low profile. The usage of these tools increases the efficiency of the campaign, especially in larger networks where it can be very time-consuming to find the logical path from the initial compromised system to the goal systems. For example, consider a multinational or government, which typically use class A-size internal networks that can contain more than 16 million IP addresses. Finding interesting systems can be hard and time-consuming if it has to be performed manually. However, in an organization with limited monitoring, simple network scanning tools can easily be used to fingerprint network services and determine functionality of systems. Each type of systems has its own "fingerprint" of available network services. For example, Windows domain controller systems have a specific combination of TCP ports 88 and 389, Linux systems have TCP port 22 open, and an Oracle database system typically uses TCP port 1521. Depending on the speed of the network, a class A network can easily be scanned in hours or days with such tools. Better yet, once interesting systems have been identified, common and freely available vulnerability and open source exploitation frameworks can be used to compromise these systems. To avoid detection, the guerilla band only needs to ensure that they use fresh attacker IP addresses and hostnames and ensure that they do not use commonly detected viruses. Since the targeted entity will only focus on the lower levels of the pyramid of pain, it will only detect an attack if computed hash values of the malicious files used by the guerilla band are common (eg, match the virus database). The part on tools and techniques provides recommendations on how to achieve this with specific techniques and tooling. However, the guerilla band should keep in mind that their actions should not be detected by alert employees or other forms of human suspicion. For example, accidentally bringing down a system because of running too much exploitation and scanning tools should be avoided at all times.

Limited monitoring

To successfully attack an entity that employs limited monitoring, the guerilla band can either determine the exact monitoring capability (eg, the inventory of monitoring tools and processes) or assume that the entity employs a higher level of monitoring. Typically, entities that have limited monitoring are focusing on the middle and lower layers of the pyramid of pain. These include atomic, computed, and sometimes behavioral attack indicators on systems and in network traffic. It is recommended that the guerilla band tries to determine the exact level of monitoring in the "reconnaissance" phase of the attack chain. A good starting point is to determine the connections between the target entity and vendors that sell security monitoring services. Social media can be used to find out which employees in the monitoring and security teams are connected with employees of security vendors.

Extensive monitoring

Due to the increase of prevention and detection capabilities, organizations have shifted the focus of IT security toward a data level: they try to determine what their most critical (data) assets are and where in their (digital) organization these are stored. However, this should not stop an effective attacker team from successfully penetrating networks and systems without being detected. An effective guerilla band can also misuse these trends. They do not need to look at the security of the individual systems; they are looking for the weakest link in the organization's complex IT environment. Luckily for the attacker, the aforementioned valuable assets can be virtually anywhere, especially in unstructured data sources: in email boxes of employees, cloud services, file servers, or smartphones. Also, in some campaigns (such as a DOS) the guerilla band does not need to gain access or manipulate these critical assets; it would suffice to prevent anyone from accessing them or achieve their goal by disrupting services and systems.

If it is required to steal or manipulate important data while staying away from centralized monitoring systems, it is recommended to not directly attack the structured data sources (such as databases or large enterprise resource systems). If more time and effort is spent during the reconnaissance and intelligence gathering phase, an attack with only a low penetration ratio can still succeed with a high exfiltration ratio. For instance, if it is determined that one individual in an organization has access to highly valuable data or assets, the attacker should focus on creating a TTP that only compromises his device(s) and use that access to steal or manipulate the assets, without deeply penetrating into the network. For example, unstructured data sources such as email or file shares can also contain valuable information for the guerilla band. Since these are less protected and monitored than structured data sources, it could be a good starting point for further attacks and penetration.

An organization that uses extensive monitoring tries to detect and prevent the specific TTPs and tools of an attacker, rather than focus on the more prevalent and obvious indicators. They do this by correlating network- and host-based indicators, gathered from all kinds of data sources in- and outside their network. If the guerilla band is to target such an organization, it is recommended to incorporate monitoring evasive techniques and distraction strategies (in case suspicion is raised with the cyber defense team) in their approach and corresponding TTPs. Distractions can be easily created, but should be used wisely as it can put the monitoring teams in higher states of alert. We will discuss relevant evasive techniques in the tools and techniques section.

Limits of encryption

Another preventive measure that organizations use to protect their data is "encryption": using a secret key to ensure that only authorized personnel with knowledge of this key can access the organizational crown jewels. However, encryption usually gives an organization a false sense of security, as it is often not correctly implemented or is insecurely configured. Therefore, the guerilla band does not have to worry about targets using encryption to protect their data. Like one of the founders of the RSA algorithm already suggested: "Cryptography usually gets bypassed, not penetrated."[g]

Organizations often give software developers responsibility over implementing information security in their applications. However, this leads to a false sense of security. Developers are usually not capable enough to deal with all possible security vulnerabilities and attack paths, especially in the field of cryptography. Implementing security protocols and cryptography is

---

[g]Source: "Turing Lecture on Cryptology: A Status Report" by Adi Shamir (2004).

science of its own. So even if at first glance an impenetrable form of encryption is used, it might still be easily reversed or bypassed.

A common example is the "encryption" of passwords in configuration files. Many applications require an authorized connection to their respective database or other connected systems. To set up this machine-to-machine connection, credentials are usually stored in a file on the application server. To protect these credentials, they are often reversibly "encrypted" or irreversibly "hashed." The latter option is not preferable as, due to the notion that a one-way hash function is considered practically impossible to invert, the application then has no way to determine the password from the hash itself. Unless the hash itself must be used to authenticate, which provides the same level of security as using a regular plain text password.

If the credentials are reversible encrypted, there must be a decryption key available to the application in memory to decrypt the password, and use it for authentication toward another system (like a database) the moment it is required. This means an attacker simply needs to either find the encryption key on disk, or in memory, which is not hard if he has access to the operating system. Simple memory injection tools exist for this purpose (such as "debuggers" or "application call sniffers"), which can be used to follow the program execution flow throughout the memory.

Also, developers often use the principle of "security through obscurity" to store authentication credentials. With this principle the security of the systems, in this case the encryption of the authentication credentials, is dependent on the secrecy of the implementation or its components itself. This is in contrast to an open encryption system, where the implementation and its components are transparent but the security of the system is dependent on the secrecy of the keys used. This is an important difference because, in case "security through obscurity" is used to store credentials, the guerilla band only needs to obtain information on how the encryption is performed rather than searching for a key. It is exactly this part that developers do wrong; they use easily reversible or weak encryption schemes. There are many examples where the password is simply encoded with algorithms like base64 (the base64 encoded string "U3VwZXJTdHIwbmdQNCQkd3BSRF8xNTI2NQ==" can easily be decoded to "SuperStr0ngP4$$w0RD_15265"). Another example is encrypting important data such as passwords with very outdated or broken ciphers, such as "ROT-13" (the ROT-13 encrypted string "FhcreFge0atC4$$j0EQ_15265" can easily be decrypted to "SuperStr0ngP4$$w0RD_15265").

It is also important to understand that encrypted data must be decrypted at some point in the execution flow from data storage to end-user representation. If this was not the case it would be impossible for end-users to work with encrypted data. The hacker group should therefore find the weakest link in this execution flow. For example, if the targeted organization or individual uses multiple forms of strong encryption, it might be easier for the guerilla band to attack the system which represents the data in an unencrypted form. Therefore, their corresponding TTP would focus on developing attacks on the end-user device, rather than attacking the (web) application, database, or underlying systems and related networks.

Even if, for example, a database uses field encryption (ie, the actual data in the database is encrypted, not only the hard disk of the underlying operating system) or the data are encrypted with encryption keys stored on specialized hardware like a hardware security module (HSM), it is still possible to obtain access. With simple attacks (like an SQL injection or weak password) it is easy to obtain unauthorized access to a database, or get access to the underlying operating system which stores the encryption keys for the database. Or, if the guerilla band obtains unauthorized access to the underlying operating system, they can modify the application code in such a way that it retrieves the encrypted data and decrypts it for them. Of course, this requires some special skill set, but that should not pose a challenge to the hacker group.

There are multiple appealing examples of bypassing encryption instead of breaking it. One of these examples is how financial transactions are handled by the Society for Worldwide Interbank Financial Telecommunication (SWIFT)[h]. SWIFT provides a network and a set of standards to enable transmission of information about financial transactions in a relatively secure way. However, on multiple occasions the SWIFT cryptographic implementations can potentially be bypassed.

Instead of attacking the (public) key infrastructure underlying the SWIFT communications network and trying to break the security of the communications between the organization and the banks, the guerilla band could, for instance, focus on obtaining access to the encryption and signing keys themselves. This may sound easier than it seems. In large organizations, these keys are typically stored in so-called "bank communication systems," which are basically regular servers (running on typical operating systems such as Windows) that have some special SWIFT software installed. Getting access to the communication encryption and transaction signing keys is a simple as obtaining high-privileged access to such a server.

Once on the server, the guerilla band actually does not even need to obtain access to the cryptographic material, which sometimes can also stored in a separate HSM. They can also modify the software or (batch) files containing

---

[h]Source: https://www.swift.com/

the payment instructions, effectively allowing for adding, modifying, or removing financial transactions without breaking the encryption and message authentication keys, or without compromising the HSM.

TOOLS AND TECHNIQUES

Tools are of utmost importance to the guerilla band as they simplify many processes and increase efficiency by automating tasks. Some tools also allow individual member of the guerilla band to collaborate more effectively, even when they are geographically distributed. Basically, every step in the presented kill chains can be aided by some form of tooling and automation. This section will describe the categories of tools that should be in the arsenal of the hacker group. Since the technique and tooling landscape is subject to rapid change, we will discuss the techniques that can be employed and the corresponding general tooling required. Remember: there is no one tool to rule them all, only human ingenuity.

Evasion techniques

Evasion techniques are used by the hacker group to disguise their actions and to ensure that their offensive actions remain undetected as long as possible. The guerilla band should test their evasion tools offline. Online testing services (that offer to scan the infected files with multiple antimalware vendors, such as Virustotal), generally share information on new/unseen infections with antimalware vendors, which could easily lead to detection in case the guerilla band uploaded their infected files to such a service. Services that promise discretion should be distrusted; providing these kinds of services provides any investigating agency with extremely valuable information. To effectively test the created malware or infection files, it is important to have information on the antimalware products used. If such information is not available, it is recommended to set up an offline testing platform, which contains software of all the major antimalware products. The newly generated malware is then analyzed by this platform to give the guerilla band an indication of the detection level. We will describe tooling to evade multiple levels and strategies of threat and virus detection.

Evading signature-based malware detection

Traditionally, host-based malware detection, or antivirus, focused on atomic or computed indicators of files on the hard disk of the host. Contemporary host-based malware detection products sometimes also focus on in-memory patterns to detect malicious behavior.

To bypass traditional host-based malware detection, multiple techniques and tools can be used. As this type of malware detection program specifically examines files on the hard disk, it can be easily bypassed by keeping the malware code in the transient (eg, RAM) memory of targeted host system. For example, abusing common (or zero-day) exploits can lead to this scenario, as they often exploit vulnerabilities which are present during runtime (eg, a buffer overflow) and thus load the exploit code in the transient memory. A disadvantage of keeping the malware code in transient memory is that it will cease to exist the moment the transient memory is reset or the hosting process is terminated. Depending on the type of infected system (server or end-user system), this can occur soon after the initial infection, for example, if the infected end-user switches off his laptop. A server, on the other hand, will typically not be reset outside regular maintenance windows. Therefore, the guerilla band has to determine whether or not they will have to make their malware code persistent, such that it will also survive a reset of the transient memory. However, making the malware code persistent such that it launches every time the operating systems starts, or even before the operating system has started (eg, by hiding the malware in the master boot record), often requires that some code has to be placed on the hard disk. This type of code is called "fully staged" (or single-staged) as it contains all functionality to launch itself after startup, after which it can set up a C2 channel back to the attacker and start postexploitation tools such as key-loggers, screen dumpers, and functionality to take control over other systems (lateral movement). Fully staged malware is often quite large (in size) and places postexploitation functionality on disk, which increases the probability of a successful detection by antivirus products. A good work-around to avoid detection is to break the malware (or payload) delivery in two or more stages.

The first stage, also called the "stager" or "dropper," is a very small program which is placed on the hard disk and does nothing more than set up a connection back to the attacker. As long as the infrastructure of the attacker (either IP addresses or hostnames) is not registered with antimalware products, a stager will raise little suspicion as many legitimate programs have similar functionality. When it succeeds in connecting back to the attack infrastructure it will download the second stage, also called the "payload stage," and places that in the transient memory of the infected machine from where it will be executed by the stager. By placing the payload stage in the transient memory, the malicious code inside is generally not scanned by the traditional antimalware products. Although the dropper is small, it still needs to be placed on hard disk and started automatically to gain persistent behavior. For example, this can be achieved by creating a service that starts with every reboot of the target, adding the program to the startup folder, loading the malicious code as a reflective Dynamic Link Library (DLL), adding an encoded autostart registry key, or creating an (Microsoft Outlook) mail filter that executes a file based on specific incoming emails.

If a dropper cannot be used, or the scenario disallows the infected target system to communicate back to the attacker and as such the malware must be stored on disk, there are other ways to evade detection: *polymorphism* and *metamorphism*. Both techniques rely on the ability to change the code of the malware while keeping the original algorithm intact, thereby misleading antimalware solutions that rely on pattern and signature matching. The code itself is changed when the malware propagates but its semantics, the meaning of the code, will not change. A simple example: both the expressions "3×3" and "$5 + 5 - 1$" will yield the same result although they use different code.

The difference between metamorphic and polymorphic malware is that metamorphic malware is completely rewritten with each iteration of execution of the malware while polymorphic malware has a static part, which stays the same with each iteration, and a dynamic part which changes with every iteration. An easy way to achieve some form of polymorphism is to modify the source code of freely available (open source) exploitation frameworks. By making changes in the templates that generate executable code, such as data appending or prepending, the signatures of the resulting malware will differ from the original ones and do not trigger simple antivirus measures. To evade more sophisticated antivirus solutions, encryption of the payload is a commonly used method. Encryption algorithms, either self-created or generally available, can be used to encrypt the main body of the payload code such that it looks meaningless to antivirus applications. However, a decrypting function and a decryption key should be added to the malware for the code to operate as intended. The moment the code gets executed (in the transient memory) on the victim, the decrypting function decrypts the encrypted code with the provided key before it is executed. If different encrypting/decrypting functions or different key pairs are used with every propagation of the malware, polymorphic behavior is obtained. This ensures that different versions of the code function the same. However, using encryption as polymorphism provides sophisticated antivirus applications with a complex signature, as the body of the virus is not altered. For example, these more sophisticated antivirus products can search for encryption and decryption patterns in the code and, while the encrypted code on disk differs with every malware sample, the malicious algorithm is equal every time the malware is executed.

Metamorphic malware is considered to be more difficult to detect as it uses multiple transformation techniques. Examples of these techniques are function reordering, program flow modification, register renaming, static data structure modification, and garbage code insertion. All these techniques can be combined, which makes detection very hard. The guerilla band should create a tool that combines these techniques such that they can be used on the fly.

Evading reputation-based malware detection

Reputation-based malware verifies the signature(s) of the files by sharing them with other products or databases, for example, by uploading them to a central online repository. Before the file or program is allowed to start, the malware solution verifies the reputation of the specific file. Uncommon files and programs generally have a lower reputation than common ones, as not many people have confirmed these as legitimate. For example, the installation file of an unknown bookkeeping product usually has a lower reputation value than the installation file of a major browser. Reputation-based detection works effectively against meta- and polymorphic malware as, due to their characteristics, these types of malware have not been used before the moment of execution and therefore automatically have a lower reputation.

It is up to the entity to set the allowed thresholds for the reputation: the boundaries that determine when a file is considered legitimate or malicious. Many organizations struggle with setting these boundaries correctly, as a too-strict boundary will result in many false positives (programs that are legitimate but considered malicious) and a too-loose boundary will result in false negatives (malicious programs that are considered legitimate). The guerilla band can use this to their advantage. In one example, we observed that the encrypted virus was detected by the reputation-based antimalware product as the computed hash was never seen on the Internet before (which logically follows from the fact that the attacker used encryption to obfuscate his payload). The attacker then embedded the staging process in a Microsoft Office macro, the macro code doing nothing more than to download and run a malicious executable in memory. The reputation-based malware agent was now unable to detect the malicious file as the Microsoft Word program has a "good" reputation and therefore was allowed to run by the antivirus program.

Evading heuristic-based malware detection

Heuristic-based malware detection focuses on detecting intrusions by monitoring the activity of systems and classifying it as normal or anomalous. The classification is often based on machine learning algorithms that use heuristics or rules to detect misuse, rather than patterns or signatures. One of its shortcomings is that it tends to have a high false positive rate, such that many legitimate actions are classified as intrusive, and that it requires useful training data, which is typically difficult to obtain in large IT environments.

Contemporary host-based malware detection products focus on in-memory patterns. Apart from heuristics, they apply techniques such as block-hashing, that computes hashes of parts of the suspicious file instead of the whole file, or are able to detect polymorphic encrypted payloads in memory.

However, these malware detection products are usually designed to search for exploitation and malware behavior, for example, code patterns that exploit a vulnerability in some software product. Although (this partly) mitigates the risk of automatic/noninteractive malware infections, such as a drive-by download of watering hole attack (which are typically triggered by exploitation of either a zero-day or well-known vulnerability), these products are less effective against malware that was launched with human interaction, for example, by tricking a targeted user to start the malware code himself during a (spear)phishing attempt. If the guerilla band detects that this type of host-based malware detection is used, it is recommended to stay away from general (automated) exploitation techniques. By actively interfering with the infected systems instead of using automatic viruses, the hacker group may cause the malware to mimic human behavior. For example, it is recommended to use impersonation attacks (eg, stealing a password) and to use regular legitimate tools and programs to perform postexploitation and lateral movement, as these are typically allowed by the antimalware solutions. For example, in a Windows environment generally available (networking) tools such as the command prompt, PowerShell, Remote Desktop, PsExec, and Windows Management Instrumentation (WMI) can be used to perform internal reconnaissance, lateral movement, and postexploitation without raising suspicion.

Evading network-based malware detection

Network-based malware detection, or intrusion detection systems, tracks specific network characteristics and monitors the network for abnormal events or trends that could indicate the presence of a threat. Examples of these characteristics include protocol usage, traffic volume, bandwidth usage, and atomic indicators such as remote hostnames and IP addresses. The anomaly detection algorithms are incorporated in physical devices (appliances) which are often placed at strategic points in the network such that they cover the traffic to and from all systems in the network. Traditional network-based anomaly detection matches the characteristics and patterns of the passing traffic through the appliance to a(n) (online) database of known attacks.

Newer network-based malware detection is based on the behavior of individual network components. Before it can be used effectively, a baseline of normal network or user behavior must be established over a certain period. Any events that do not match the baseline are flagged as anomalous. Another important feature of these detection devices is the usage of virtual environments to test possible malicious files. These network-based antimalware solutions monitor the network traffic for all executable files downloaded by users of the entity. Unrecognized or uncommon files are automatically extracted from the network traffic and executed in a separate virtual environment (a so-called "sandbox"), which is set up on the fly, to determine what the file is actually doing. Properties such as resources used, connections made, and execution behavior are inspected for malicious intent.

To bypass these kinds of products, the guerilla band can use multiple tactics. One easy way to increase the detection difficulty is to use encrypted channels, for delivering the attack as well as utilizing the C2 structure. For example, if all C2 traffic from the infected system to infrastructure controlled by the hacker group is encrypted, network-based detection systems cannot easily break the encrypted channel and inspect the individual packets. Although some entities have implemented so-called "SSL offloaders," systems that are able to inspect HTTPS encrypted packets, these products are expensive and require changes to the internal Public Key Infrastructure (PKI) structure of an entity. Furthermore, the guerilla band can implement an additional encryption layer, on top of the "normal" HTTPS protocol, which makes it harder to inspect the packets and detect infiltrations.

Another tactic the hacker group can employ to decrease the detection probability is to mislead these devices by emulating nonmalicious behavior. For example, as the network intrusion detection systems start a virtual environment to test the possible malicious files, the guerilla band can program the virus in such a way that it detects if it is executed in a virtual environment. If that is the case, the malware is programmed to not do anything malicious. Another way to trick these kinds of network appliances is to wait for user input, movement of the mouse or keyboard, which indicates that a human is opening the file (instead of an analysis algorithm in a virtual environment). Also, as the network appliances cannot keep the virtual environment open for too long because of restrictions on resource usage, the malware can be programmed to wait for a specified amount of time before the malicious behavior is activated. In practice, 1 day is usually enough. But, the most beneficial tactic we have observed in practice is to create malware that only sets up a connection to the attacker-controlled server over a nonsuspicious channel such as HTTP, waiting for malicious commands to be executed. The moment the virus is analyzed, nothing malicious can be found. However, when a human operator, that is, a member of the hacker group, has verified that it is an actual user unwittingly opening and installing the malware, the payload stage can be remotely activated and the malware can reveal its real purpose, beyond the reach of the intrusion detection system.

To cope with these shortcomings, newer network intrusion detection products can be integrated with so-called "Security Information and Event Management" (SIEM) systems, which gather anomalies and possible indicators from multiple sources to correlate these and create one consistent threat overview. However, even if these SIEM implementations are used, the guerilla band can still employ evasive tactics. One of these tactics is to infect and operate systems outside the reach of the SIEM implementation. To reduce the number of events and corresponding incidents generated, many SIEM implementations only focus on centralized systems such as proxies, DNS, network components, Active Directory, email, antivirus, and important servers. Although these systems are usually targets for the hacker group, they can minimize the effort and time spent on attacking them. For example, if the highest privileges within a Windows Active Directory domain (so-called "domain administrator" privileges) are required to execute a TTP, it is recommended to hunt for these credentials on less important servers, outside the reach of the central security monitoring implementations. Once high-privileged access is obtained and an administrator can be impersonated, regular administrative tools can be used to attack the important systems. Usage of these tools by an impersonated administrator does raise less suspicion than attacking the monitored systems directly.

Another tactic is to flood the centralized monitoring systems with events, hoping that the security team would handle successive events as "false positive." For example, not all SIEM solutions support or have log source authentication enabled. This means that the correlation system does not verify the identity of the log source and authenticity of the sender (in this case a monitored system). The guerilla band can misuse this to flood or spoof log messages and security events, thereby creating too many alerts and rendering the SIEM environment ineffective. Although this does raise much suspicion with the security teams, we have observed in practice that they could not effectively cope with the number of events, which in the end disguised real malicious events. Another example is that allegedly Russian hackers used to launch DDOS attacks at banks when they were transferring large amounts of money to evade detection by the security team.

Evading hunting teams

Some more mature organizations have adopted the notion of "assume breach": a security strategy that represents a cultural shift and methodology. These organizations base their security strategy, principles, processes, and technology on the assumption that attackers already exploited vulnerabilities, infected their network, gained privileged access, and made active use of persistent C2 structures. For these organizations, security operations is not just about passive monitoring, but also actively employing highly skilled defensive specialists that search for correlation of different log events, security alerts, and determining the context of breaches, sometimes aided by machine learning algorithms. These specialists have the task to separate the indicators of compromise from the indicators of attack and develop a strategy to delay the threat actors before they have determined a way to completely remove them. Groups of these specialists are called "hunting teams."

The most effective way to evade hunting teams is trivial: do not attract their attention. However, as an attacker you have little control on what actions will be detected or what will attract the hunting team's attention. Therefore, two other strategies can be applied. The first strategy is to use the time the hunting team requires to detect and react to the threat as efficiently as possible. In defensive teams, these time windows are called the "(mean) time to detect" and "(mean) time to respond." If the hacker group is detected, it does not mean that their mission is fully compromised. There still might be enough time to complete the mission and, more importantly, cover their tracks.

Depending on the governance structure, size of the organization, and skills of the hunting teams, this can provide the guerilla band with an additional timeframe of hours or days. Also, hunting teams often do not have a complete overview of the risk, impact, and scope of the guerilla's actions the first time the team detects suspicious behavior. Before they can initiate triage, clean up, or execute other responsive actions, a well-planned and prepared guerilla campaign can be still be completed before its access from the systems is removed. Hunting teams do not always have the mandate to shut down the infected/compromised system(s) immediately, which can also provide the guerilla band with a sufficiently large window of opportunity to complete their goal. However, before they initiate any actions, the guerilla band needs to determine if their targeted organization has employed hunting teams, as this might heavily influence their preparation process and related TTPs.

The second strategy to evade a hunting team is to mislead them. This works especially well in large IT environments where infections, malware, and even advanced persistent threats are "business as usual." In such an environment, hunting teams deal with (large-scale) attacks on a daily basis. The guerilla band can use this to its advantage as the hunting teams are busy enough dealing with all kinds of attacks. It is therefore recommended that the guerilla band develops two different types of TTPs: one to complete their mission and one to mislead the hunting team. These TTPs should be executed simultaneously or shortly after each other and should be as different as possible. They should not only differ in terms of infrastructure, tools, and exploits used, but also in terms of motive and goal. This will prevent the hunting team from correlating both of the developed scenarios, which might expose the guerilla band and its motives. It is important that the TTP that misleads the hunting team consumes their time as much as possible. Therefore, it should be easy enough for them to discover, but hard enough to determine impact, scope, and motive.

Network scanning tools

To perform external and internal reconnaissance of available infrastructure components, network scanning tools can be used. These tools do nothing more than enumerate systems and services, and in doing so, they can quickly give an overview of connected systems, especially when the hacker group encounters a new, unknown network. The challenge in using network scanning tools is to decrease the scanning time. Often the guerilla band will find themselves in the position where they have to scan a large network in a short amount of time. Networks consisting of 16 million IP addresses, with every IP address potentially having more than 100,000 network services available, are not unusual. It is recommended that the hacker group configures their network scanning tools in such a way that they first scan the most important services, for example, the services that are known to contain security issues. When the hacker group has an overview of those, they can commence with weaponization and delivery of the first attacks while still scanning the other services.

Mapping tools for (internal) reconnaissance

Mapping tools can be used to map the infrastructure and system components to vulnerable exploitable services. The guerilla band should try to map all of the functional levels of the IT environment (such as ERP systems, databases, storage systems, file shares, email systems, and network components). For example, in many organizations the security of middleware (products and services such as Tomcat, JBoss, Websphere, PHP, Java Remote Method Invocation, etc.) is often overlooked as the infrastructure maintenance teams perceive it as a task for the application maintenance teams and vice versa. Therefore, it is a good starting point to map these middleware products to vulnerabilities. Common security issues with these products are outdated software and default/weak passwords. These can be exploited by the guerilla band to gain control over the underlying operating system, even if that layer has been fully patched. In this case, the tool itself should scan the internal infrastructure fingerprinting the middleware services based on the combination of open ports—for example, Tomcat usually uses TCP port 8080 whereas JBoss uses TCP port 8083 and 1098—and afterward probe these services for the version number and try predefined usernames and password combinations on the management interface.

Like the middleware example, the hacker group should develop, buy, or download tools that perform these kinds of scanning activities for all the functional system groups and levels of the IT environment.

Password cracking tools

During many cyber intrusions, the guerilla band will find themselves in a position that they have obtained access to some form of password storage, but the passwords themselves are scrambled through a form of cryptography, often a one-way hashing function. This hashing function usually is defined through a mathematical function that irreversibly stores the password. For example, in a Windows environment the hash values of the LAN Manager (LM) and New Technology LAN Manager (NTLM) algorithms for the password "Sup3rS3cure" are "3E9CB63E11A812CB0A13EEA078BCAE83" and "10D15E13DA239A9B9BFE9C0B957EB894" respectively. In a Unix environment, the hash value of the SHA-512 crypt algorithm (ie, the hash starts with the identifier "6") for the same password would be "6aNybBvRSaz4I.5aBG.vt8sQPKbuewwMZ9OACeOR7Aw5tNVZcMvF7ou14eDGqS11EevJelvviZ25r-JRW9B5D10." - Please note that in this example the "salt" "2173a585" is used. A *salt* is public random data that are appended to the password before it is scrambled, to prevent different users with the same password from being identified by just inspecting the corresponding hash values. If in a Windows-based environment an LM hash is obtained, it can be easily cracked within hours, as the LM protocol cannot handle passwords longer than seven characters. Any password longer than seven character will be split after seven characters, the resulting two phrases hashed apart, and both hashes pasted to each other again. Even if complex characters, digits, and capitals are used, an attacker can still easily crack two 7-character passwords on a regular laptop within a day.

Apart from some situations where the obtained password hash can be used as an authentication credential itself (ie, the previously described pass-the-hash technique), the guerilla band needs to find the plain-text form of the password before they can use it to authenticate. Although many password cracking tools are freely available, they all work in the same way. They perform an exhaustive search by generating candidate passwords, apply the hash function, and compare the result with the obtained password hash. The time required to iterate over all the candidate passwords is linear with the password cracking speed. Although recent advances in hardware increase the cracking speed, they cannot cope with the increase of password length, which exponentially increases the time required to crack a password. For example, except if the targeted entity uses the NTLM algorithm, cracking passwords longer than 10 characters quickly becomes an infeasible process. Therefore, it is of utmost importance that the guerilla band does not focus on increasing the cracking speed, but focuses on the creating and maintaining good lists of candidate passwords, the so-called "word lists." We observed that when cultural and linguistic aspects, such as language and keyboard layout of the targeted entity, are taken into account when creating word lists, many more passwords could be cracked than when using regular word lists. For example, consider that an employee of the entity "Acmecompany" has the password "Acmecompany1234!" The corresponding password hash is not easily brute forced as the password consists of 16 characters, including digits and a special character. However, a guerilla band who creates a word list containing candidate passwords formed with the company name and predictable sets of special characters has a very high probability of success to retrieve the password.

Miscellaneous tools

Apart from the tools mentioned, there are other tools that can be of aid to the guerilla band:

- Protocol and software fuzzers, to find indicators for buffer overflows which can lead to the identification of zero-day vulnerabilities.
- SQL-injection mappers, that automatically verify web application parameters for possible SQL-injection attacks.
- C2 frameworks, that help set up a structure to communicate with compromised machines.
- Packet capturing tools, that retrieve network data packets for analysis.
- Collaboration tools, to provide a framework where multiple members of the hacker group can share information securely.
- Exploitation frameworks, to gather, develop, and share exploits among members of the guerilla band.

EFFECTS

This chapter has covered how to gather information required for conducting operations and the TTPs used in these operations. As mentioned in Chapter 1, actions alone do not amount to ascertaining the goals of the hacker group. Those waging cyber guerilla conduct operations to sequentially attain (sub)goals to achieve a predefined end-state. In other words, operations are means to an end and every action should have purpose.

The TTPs or means and methods described previously can be used for a wide variety of purposes. A DDOS can be used to coerce an opponent into performing the hacker group's will or be used to render a server inoperable for an amount of time. As the hacker group should be aware of the variety of effects which can be attained via their means and methods, this section will discuss potential effects. In doing so, this section deviates from Che Guevara's approach, which focuses primarily on physical effects: destruction of and denying access to infrastructure (eg, war industry) and physically influencing (ie, population) or injuring persons (ie, state agents). This section aims to provide a more comprehensive range of effects.

Cyber guerilla is waged by nonstate actors and as such may shy away from effects-based thinking as it is practiced by state actors (eg, armed forces). Using effects to streamline hacker group efforts, however, can greatly improve matching operations and activities to hacker group goals. For instance, a hacker group aiming to influence an opponent could simply go for a target-based approach and indicate they "want to hack a web server." It is paramount, however, that the group specifies internally—either implicitly or explicitly—what the purpose is of hacking the web server.

Hacking for the sake of hacking, without filtering and selecting potential venues of attack, will increase the chance of the hacker group being profiled, compromised, and eventually neutralized. In other words, when contemplating operations, cyber guerillas should not focus on the target (eg, the web server) but keep in mind the intended effect (eg, denying the opponent the ability to express themselves to the public via their web server). The former will result in tunnel vision focusing on the target; the latter will provide a more comprehensive overview of ways to achieve the intended effect.

Overview of effects

This section will now turn to potential effects that can be achieved via operations; as any categorization, this overview is arbitrary and nonexhaustive. There are cognitive/behavioral effects and the more traditional physical effects. The most relevant cognitive effects in the context of cyber guerilla are inform, mislead, and cognitively degrade. The relevant physical effects are deny, disrupt, degrade, and destroy.

Inform

The effect "inform" is aimed at the population, which might have a supportive, neutral, or hostile stance toward the hacker group. An activity aimed at informing the population aims to gain support for the hacker group's cause and degrade the support for the opponent. These activities may include the use of social media, mailings, texts, and the conventional media. This media presence should be firmly maintained by the members dedicated to external communication (see Chapter 2).

When a hacker group sees an opportunity to exploit success via exposure, for instance when the hacker group uncovers compromising data during an operation, they can choose to use this information to degrade support for the opponent. If such a target of opportunity is not present and the hacker group seeks exposure to further their goal, the hacker group can conduct an action aimed at getting attention and inform the public about their presence. These actions do not require intrusions in systems containing the opponent's crown jewels; low-hanging fruit can be equally effective to draw attention to the hacker group. For example, "hacking" an organization's official social media account, or exposing personally identifiable information of high-ranking officials, can be equally effective. Whether a target of opportunity or preplanned, seeking attention should be a conscious decision since it will also make the opponent and other actors aware of the hacker group, for instance law enforcement and intelligence agencies.

Mislead

The effect "mislead" is aimed at the opponent and other actors such as law enforcement, intelligence agencies, security firms, and hunting teams. These are activities aimed at throwing dust in the opponents' eyes, to create a sort of artificial fog of war, to make them believe things which are not there. This is essential for a hacker group, by misleading the opponent they focus their considerable resources on wrong locations (virtual and physical). As the opponent focuses on that location, the hacker group can strike more easily in other locations. The hacker group could, for instance, mislead an opponent by conducting a DOS attack on infrastructure to cover up another activity, by planting false clues (eg, alter log files with fake credentials), purposefully making "mistakes" (eg, trigger IDS, IPS, and honeypots), and leaking information regarding the next attack target (eg, disclosing target IPs on social media or Pastebin-type websites). Misleading an actor requires intricate knowledge about the controls present in the target infrastructure and procedures in place for reporting incidents.

Cognitively degrade

Degradation can be both a cognitive and physical effect; in the sense of the former, the effect "degrade" is aimed at reducing an actor's morale, perception, and attitude. This can be achieved via direct and indirect ways. A direct way of achieving this is would be sending messages (eg, email, text, instant message, social media) to specific officials trying to influence them. As with any form of targeted communication, the more details the likelier that the message will be deemed credible and will affect the target's psyche. The hacker group could take different approaches to influence the opponent's employees; both coercive and more nuanced messages can attain an effect. For instance, the hacker group could threaten or coerce an employee with repercussions when they keep performing services for the opponent. Even if the target still goes to work normally, his morale will be affected by the threat, that is, if it is perceived as a credible one. A more nuanced way of affecting an opponent's personnel is sending them messages or drawing their attention to messages which unveil the missteps of their employer. If these messages are well written and contain credible statements, personnel might start doubting the intentions of their employer and may start asking questions.

An indirect way of degrading the opponent is by aiming to turn their network against them. Instead of directly targeting the opponent, the hacker group will target their peers and other influential actors in their surroundings. This can be done, for example, by leaking legitimate or false compromising information about the actor and its personnel onto the web or sending targeted messages to the opponent's network highlighting the flaws of the opponent. Another potential way of eroding support indirectly is a false-flag operation. A false-flag operation is aimed at making actor "A" believe that he is attacked by actor "B" while actor "C" was actually responsible for planning and executing the attack. In the context of cyber guerilla, if the hacker group, actor C, has access to B's infrastructure it can use this infrastructure to attack actor A. As A is assuming that B attacked him he will act against actor B, for instance by reporting the incident with law enforcement agencies, thereby degrading the trust between the two actors.

Deny, disrupt, and degrade

Whereas cognitive effects are aimed at eroding support for and the morale of the opponent, the more "traditional" effects (deny, disrupt, degrade, deceive, and destroy) are aimed at reducing the effectiveness of the opponent in conducting activities by targeting assets required for their activities. Although there is a doctrinal difference between deny, disrupt, and degrade, they are very similar. A business process can be *disrupted* by *denying* infrastructure or services and as such the process as a whole can be *degraded*. This section will choose degrade to pertain to these type of effects, the degradation of a function of the opponent.

An example is degrading the ability of the opponent to organize themselves by targeting the office environment, for instance by manipulating mail servers. This may degrade the opponent's ability to organize themselves and to synchronize efforts for countering the hacker group. Another example of degradation of the opponent's capabilities is blocking their (social) media accounts, by doing so the opponent's ability to communicate is degraded. Besides these there are many other possible courses of action that will degrade certain parts of the opponent's organization (eg, degradation of their logistics, finance, office infrastructure, production environment, and supply chain).

Destroy

The effect "destroy" encompasses the destruction of an opponent's ability to collect, process, store, and disseminate information. Although destruction will result in a degradation of an opponent's capability, it differs from the effect "degrade" as to the reversibility of the effect. Destruction is about rendering a target useless beyond repair or renewal, whereas degradation is about temporarily reducing functions of the opponent, that is, for the time of the conflict of interest between the hacker group and the opponent. For instance, a DOS attack against a mail server will result in a temporal disruption of the mail service. Destruction of the opponent's mail system would entail, among other, wiping mail servers, address databases, and workstations to an extent they are rendered unbootable. The opponent would be forced to engage in an extensive recovery process which may or may not include acquiring new infrastructure to replace the compromised systems.

Destruction of an opponent's functions can be a viable course of action for the hacker group, for instance to cover up traces of an incursion on a system. At the same time it is very labor-intensive to truly destroy a function or infrastructure without physically destroying hardware. Besides that, when destroying infrastructure the hacker group forfeits the possibility to usurp the compromised infrastructure and stored information into their own assets. Also, destroying infrastructure will most certainly draw attention to the hacker group as the opponent will most likely request help from law enforcement and information security companies to forensically determine what has happened.

MEDIA STRATEGY

As described in Chapter 1, cyber guerilla can only be truly effective with the support of the public. Without public support the hacker group can still conduct operations but these will have little to no effect outside the affected target. A hacker group lacking support may be able to influence the state and other actors via cyber guerilla tactics, but without support they will be "just another hacker collective." To gain momentum or support, the hacker group may decide to actively promote the narrative overarching their activities, in other words, explain why they are conducting operations. This exposure may result in new recruits, active supporters, and even financial support. The hacker group may reach out to its surroundings via

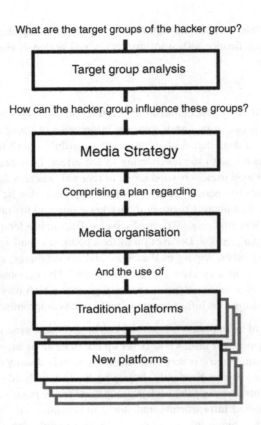

What are the target groups of the hacker group?

Target group analysis

How can the hacker group influence these groups?

Media Strategy

Comprising a plan regarding

Media organisation

And the use of

Traditional platforms

New platforms

■ **FIGURE 3.3**

conventional media (newspapers, magazines, pamphlets, etc.) and relatively new media (Facebook, Twitter, Linkedin, RenRen, email, instant messaging services, text, multiplayer gaming, etc.). Before being able to do so in an effective manner, the hacker group should think through their media strategy (Fig. 3.3) This section will expand on effectively utilizing media to gain support and to deny support to the opponent. It will discuss (1) the media organization in the hacker group, (2) considerations for communicating with targets, and (3) a brief overview of means and methods.

Media organization within the hacker group

There are multiple scenarios in which the hacker group should deliberate on seeking exposure. This may happen after an operation, for example, the hacker group has had operational success and sees an opportunity to exploit this success even further. Another scenario is being confronted with media during an operation, for instance as a result of operational compromise or the opponent seeking media attention. The hacker group may also have conducted a preplanned operation deliberately seeking media attention to create exposure.

Whether it is planned (pre- or ad hoc) or unplanned, the decision to seek exposure or respond to inquiries should be a conscious one. As a result of exposure, the hacker group will become known to the public, opponent, and a variety of other actors (law enforcement, intelligence agencies, security companies, etc.). Despite the downsides of seeking exposure, it can be a viable way for furthering the hacker group goals. The hacker group should, however, tread carefully and think through their media strategy. There are many more possible scenarios for seeking media attention; the main distinguishing characteristic is whether it is (1) planned by the hacker group or (2) forced upon them.

In the case of planned media attention, whether it is ad hoc or a preplanned part of their strategy, the hacker group has most likely already dedicated one or more members to the external communication task. As described in Chapter 2, this external communication task should focus on using media to further the hacker group's goals. This can be aimed at mobilizing support for the hacker group, denying the opponent support, or generally shaping certain target audiences. The member tasked with external communication should be the one assisting in creating a media strategy; keeping track of the "buzz" surrounding the hacker group; interacting with supporting, neutral, and hostile actors; and creating the content for the various channels. Besides that, this member should aim to create awareness in the other hacker group members regarding the narrative of the group and how to deal with inquiries. Different or incompatible storylines told by different members of the same group will hurt the credibility of the group and may be exploited by an opponent.

The other scenario is a situation where media attention is forced upon the hacker group; this situation is not about exploiting the media to the benefit of the hacker group, it is about damage control. When media attention is forced upon the hacker group, the group might feel that they should respond very rapidly to inquiries and task members to external communication on the go. This is perhaps the least effective thing to do; it will result in a haphazard media organization, inconsistent statements, and uncertainty within hacker group members. Although timely internal communication (to the hacker group members) and external communication (to the inquirers) is essential, the first step for leadership should be to take a step back, get a grasp of the situation, and assess the possibilities open to the hacker group.

If the hacker group decides to respond to the media attention, which is an option and not a requirement, they should put forward a spokesperson as a single point of contact for the outside world. This spokesperson, depending on the context, can be supported by other hacker group members. Apart from appointing a single point of contact for inquirers, the hacker group should decide which channels to use for communicating with the media. The hacker group does not necessarily have to respond to all inquiries since this would be a very labor-intensive activity. Instead, the hacker group should select those channels best suited to mitigate the effect of the compromise. Although the situation is different, planned and unplanned media attention make use of the same means and methods for influencing actors.

Considerations

Effective external communication is hard, primarily due to the complicated nature of human communication and machine assisted communication. Communication can best be understood by using one of the most fundamental models: Shannon's components of message transfer. This model comprises the essential components of communication: the information source (a database), a transmitter (a device to send the message), a channel (a network across which the message can be sent), a receiver (a device to receive the message), and a destination (the person for whom the message is intended).

Before being able to select the information source, transmitter, and channel best suited to create an effect within an actor or audience, the intended audience has to be understood—both the receiver and destination. People have different online presences, some are "all over the web" with social media, mail addresses, phone numbers, addresses, while some are "Google-proof" to some extent; that is, they have a very minimal virtual footprint. As with any action taken to influence people, it is essential to understand the intended audience and assign the most effective media to attain a particular effect. Analyzing the target actor for media purposes is called target group analysis in traditional marketing or target audience analysis in military terms. It comprises the activities aimed at attaining the information needed to understand the target audience to tailor influence attempts to the specific audience.

The goal of target group analysis is segmenting large heterogeneous groups into smaller parts to be able to influence them more effectively. Segmenting factors that could be taken into account are geographic (nations, states, regions, counties, cities, or even neighborhoods), demographic (age, life cycle stage, gender, income, occupation, education, religion, ethnicity, and

generation), psychographic (social class, lifestyle, or personality characteristics), and behavioral (occasions, benefits, user status, usage rate, loyalty
status).[i]

While it is possible to analyze virtual target groups manually, this is a
very labor-intensive activity. There is an increasing amount of free online
tools to (semi)automatically generate online target group insights. Tools
such as Topsy, Social Mention, and Google Alerts generate insights in a
brand's online performance. These tools can be used by the hacker group to
gain insights in the online sentiment (buzz) surrounding the hacker group.
Depending on the tools, these insights can capture almost any aspect of
online behavior: sentiment at a given time, location, relationship status,
financial status, social network(s), employment history, education, political
preferences, sexual preferences, shopping habits, devices used to browse the
Internet, IP address, MAC address, and many more.

The target group insights serve to select the most effective message, transmitter, and channel for a specific receiver and destination (target group).
Different target groups are receptive to different forms of engagement.
Those without smartphones (receiver) cannot receive Whatsapp (channel)
messages; those without a Twitter profile cannot receive Tweets directed at
them; those without a phone number cannot be phoned. Engaging a target
group has become a great deal more complicated than before; there are considerably more transmitters/encoders, receivers/decoders, and channels. As
a consequence of the complexity, target group analysis is more important
than ever.

Before being able to engage and influence humans virtually, one
must know what devices they are using to send and receive messages
("encoder"/"decoder" in Fig. 3.4), what channels they are using (Fig. 3.4,
eg, Tumblr, Facebook, Instagram, Linkedin, Mail, Pinterest, YouTube,
Google + , RenRen, Xing, Short Message Service, Vine, Whatsapp, regular
telephone or VoIP telephone). These types of channels have different means
of expressing messages, for instance via video (eg, YouTube and Vine),
image (eg, Pinterest and Instagram), written text (eg, Tumblr, Whatsapp,
SMS), audio (eg, telephone), or a combination thereof (Facebook, Twitter,
Linkedin, RenRen, Xing, etc.).

Communication or engagement does not take place in splendid isolation;
there are complicating factors such as personal context, situational context,
and different types of noise (Fig. 3.4). The personal and situational context

---

[i]Armstrong, Gary and Philip Kotler. *Marketing: An Introduction.* 12th ed. London: Pearson
Education, 2015, p. 199.

Situational context

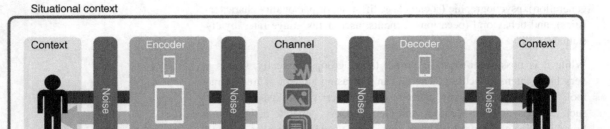

■ FIGURE 3.4

can be affected by physical, cultural, psychological, and historical factors. When, for instance, somebody tries to communicate with a person in a crowded room the physical context (noise, crowded, limited vision, etc.) can impair the effectiveness of the message. Communicating without taking note of certain norms (cultural context) may result in the person taking offense and ignoring the message. Trying to intimidate someone via a message may or may not impede effectiveness of the message (social–emotional context); safe to say is that such a message will have an impact on the receptiveness to future messages (historical context). These factors should be taken into account when communicating with the audience surrounding the hacker group.

Apart from context as complicating factor there is noise, which comprises all things that interfere with the message being accurately sent and received. Four types of noise can occur at any time when communicating, namely: physical, physiological, psychological, and semantic noise. Physical noise can occur when a connection is severed or impaired by a malfunctioning channel or encoder/decoder (eg, faulty hardware or software). Physiological noise could occur when the receiver is not able to read the information on his screen or other medium due to physical impairments or their physical well-being. Psychological noise affects the effectiveness of the message's content due to the receiver's biases, preferences, and feelings toward the message or the sender. Semantic noise captures the sender's inability to properly create a message that can be understood by the receiver, for instance a message containing language that is too specialized (abbreviations, technical terms, etc.) or wrongly formulated (wrong language, grammar, etc.).

Understanding a target group's preferred encoders/transmitters, decoder/receivers, channels, situational context, personal context, and potential noise is imperative for effective target group engagement by the hacker group. These aspects should ideally be taken into account before engaging a target group. Most of the time, however, this is a process of trial and error based on partial understanding of the target group. As target groups are diverse, noise sources are very diverse, and contexts are even more diverse, describing the means and methods (the channels) for influencing specific target groups is a daunting challenge. The following sections will describe some illustrative channels (means and methods) for influencing target groups.

New media

This section will discuss how relatively new media can be used to further the goals of the hacker group. It will provide practical and conceptual footholds for the hacker group planning to use the following channels: social media, email, instant messaging, text messages, forums, blogs, and other capabilities.

Using social media

Social media can be used for four activities: listening (or consuming), reacting (or curating), producing (or creating), and interacting (or collaborating). Before being able to effectively carry out any of these activities the hacker group should create social media profiles. A good starting point is to create these first on popular social networking sites—Twitter, Facebook, YouTube—and then gradually create more on other less popular platforms. Even if the hacker group has no desire to engage in social media, they should at least safeguard the organizational names on the most popular social media to prevent somebody from misusing their name. Once the accounts are created, the hacker group can engage in the different social media activities, which will be described in the following section.

Listening is very similar to target group analysis; it is about understanding the online sentiment (the "buzz") regarding a particular issue and the actors engaged in an issue area. Understanding buzz is made easy by aforementioned social media monitoring tools. After understanding the environment—having listened, the hacker group could take steps to react to content created by others, for instance correct erroneous facts, rectify a situation, or concur with a post. A next step in using social media is creating own content. The format (text, video, or audio) of the content depends on the platform used. For example, Facebook, LinkedIn, and Twitter can facilitate any of these formats while Instagram and Vine use images and videos. The hacker group should tailor their content to the specific platform; simply copying content or copiously cross-referencing impairs the effectiveness of a message.

By reacting and creating content the hacker group can build a virtual community and will gain a foothold in the buzz surrounding their issue areas. In the beginning stages of building a media presence the hacker group should have modest expectations toward media attention. Some overenthusiastic adopters of social media think it is possible to become the next viral "post" on social media overnight. This is far from true and happens rarely; in most cases the hacker group has to become trustworthy and worthy of following before being capable of generating (viral) growth. Another misconception is that everybody will read the content posted on the freshly created profile; again, first you will have to build a community—for example, consisting of followers, fans, or subscribers—around the hacker group profiles.

Once the hacker group succeeds at building trust and a community, it will become apparent that the community is a rich resource of information, ideas, and support. Interaction with the community is key for harvesting this information; asking the community for feedback and collaboration in establishing goals can further the goals of the hacker group. Contrary to what some think, online communities accept and appreciate when a hacker group asks, what do you want us to do? Or what do you need? Can you help us?

Apart from the activities of listening, reacting, creating, and interacting, many actors engage in measuring the effectiveness of their online campaigns. The online activities on social media can be analyzed over time by using variables such as brand influence, followers, mentions, reposted content, positive or negative mentions, reach, etc. These variables or metrics are analyzed in data mining like tools and graphically represented in dashboards. This can be very helpful to evaluate the effectiveness of online activities conducted by the hacker group; it should not, however, be the prime purpose of engaging with online communities. Metrics offer insights and can contribute to understanding, but on the other hand it is but a graphic, oversimplified representation of reality and prone to errors, misconfigurations, and human error.

Using mail

The hacker group can also engage with target groups using email, that is, if the mail addresses of individuals belonging to the target group are known. These types of informative emails are different from the offensive ones described previously in this chapter (eg, spear phishing). Here, email is used to inform and win over target groups by convincing them of the hacker group's narrative. Finding mail addresses is easy, as many people litter mail addresses across the web, for example, on company websites or social media profiles. Unfortunately, these people are not necessarily the ones belonging to a particular target group for an organization. There are some good practices of getting the mail addresses, for instance by putting an email sign-up box prominently on hacker group platforms or renting lists of consumer names.

Important to realize is that the target group receives copious amounts of mails and deems a large portion of those to be spam. If a receiver decides the mail is not relevant (psychological noise) or is considered spam by the spam filters (physical or "logical" noise), the message will most likely not be read. The user decides in seconds whether the mail is relevant; hence the mail should have a strong subject and opening line and a clear call to action.

Using instant messaging

Instant messaging platforms such as Whatsapp, Facebook Messenger, WeChat, Line, and Viber can also be used by the hacker group to engage target groups. These platforms enable the creation of private chat rooms with single or multiple individuals on the basis of a mobile phone number or social media account. Before being able to engage with the target groups the hacker group has to connect on social media with the target group (building online presence) or find out their phone numbers. Some people are listed in white- and yellow-page phonebooks with their mobile number, others have their mobile number listed in their social media profile, and there are some who have no public record of their mobile number. An organization could take the same type of actions as with getting mail addresses to learn the numbers of the target audience (eg, subscribe to a instant message service, provide incentives for subscription, rent mobile phone lists, etc.). Contrary to mail, instant messaging is closer to real-time communication; after having received a message the receiver is prompted to open and read the message.

Text messages

Although very similar to instant messaging, short messaging service (SMS) uses the voice network and as such is an (almost) universal service. Every mobile phone with a cellular signal can send and receive text messages while instant messaging can only be done on smartphones connected to the Internet. Text messages offer no possibilities to add media (audio, images, videos). A protocol offering this functionality is Multimedia Messaging Service (MMS), which is often integrated in proprietary mobile operating systems (eg, Apple's Message app). But this, logically, requires more bandwidth and thereby negates the universality of SMS. Contrary to instant messaging, group chats are not integrated in SMS applications; hence it primarily serves one-to-one communication. There are, however, solutions for sending SMS messages to groups of contacts. Before being able to do so, a hacker group needs to find out the phone numbers within the target group; ways of finding these out have been described (in the section about instant messaging).

Forums

Another channel is forums or community bulletin boards, which are discussion sites. A forum provides a place for online discussion on a particular issue area. When conducting target group analyses, it may become apparent that the target group is engaged in a particular forum. Apart from being a rich source of information regarding topics of interest of a particular target group, the forum can also serve as a channel. The hacker group can react and interact with individuals regarding specific issues of interest. Dedicated forums, not being facilitated by social media, often require separate credentials; hence a hacker group needs to create a profile before being able to engage others via these forums. Forums can be used constructively the same as mail, but forums are also excellent for destructive effects via trolls, flame wars, forum spamming, and other malicious activities.

Blogs

Web logs or blogs are online journals with posts (image, video, or text) that express ideas and thoughts. Although blogs can be used for internal communication within the hacker group, this section focuses on the use of blogs for external communication. Blogs can be used for various purposes by the hacker group, for instance explaining the narrative of the hacker group, slandering the opposing actor, and explaining what the hacker group has done or uncovered during an operation. The hacker group can draw attention to blog updates via Really Simple Syndication (RSS), social media, mailings, or other channels. Many people respond to the author of the blog with feedback, contrasting views, and other comments; this form of collaboration could result in increased understanding of the hacker group's online audience.

Multiplayer gaming[j]

Apart from the more or less conventional social media platforms, the hacker groups can also use other digital platforms to spread the message. There are several virtual social environments with millions of users, for instance SecondLife, which is one of the oldest and most popular virtual social environments. Other online social environments include not

---

[j]The authors are indebted to Guido Blaauw for providing the insights required for writing the section on multiplayer gaming.

only IMVU, Club Cooee, Planet Calypso, Habbo Hotel, and Kaneva but also multiplayer games such as World of Warcraft but also Call of Duty, Battlefield, and GTA. These virtual worlds can be used for discussion, training, and even passing funds between members or supporters without a trace.

Other online capabilities

The previous sections have described how the hacker group can use websites, social media, blogs, instant messaging, and text messaging to influence target audiences. There are, of course, many other capabilities not covered here that could affect virtual personas; this section, for instance, has not covered Wikis, Podcasts, Vlogs, livecasting, or photo sharing. These capabilities, however, resemble the capabilities described previously which are the most illustrative ones for a range of capabilities.

Using conventional media

The following section will briefly discuss using the conventional media to influence target groups. This section is not about offensively gaining access to the media, as gaining access to systems—which may include those of the media—was already covered in this chapter. Instead, this section will describe how to use the media's desire for the next scoop and exclusive story to the benefit of the hacker group. It will discuss the following channels: telephone, television, newspapers/magazines, radio, and online news websites.

Telephone

Despite the unprecedented use of mail, voice communication often overshadows mail's effectiveness in impact upon the receiver. Voice communication, irrespective of the medium, over IP or via the plain old telephone system (POTS), is still a viable and effective way of communicating with selected individuals from target audiences. Although it is possible to call multiple persons at a time, telephone is best suited for one-to-one communication; reaching out to larger target groups via phone calls will be a very labor-intensive activity. Hence, the hacker group, when deliberating on phone campaigns, should select whom to call. The most viable method for phone campaigns is selecting key players in a target group. By influencing these key players, the hacker group can win them for the hacker group's cause and potentially gain the support of the extensive network of the key player. This saves the hacker group time and can be equally or even more effective than reaching out to every individual in a target group.

Television, radio, newspapers/magazines, online news websites

This section will discuss the following conventional channels: television, radio, newspapers/magazines, and online news websites. Although very different in form, the method of exploiting these to the hacker group's benefit is the same. There are two options when deliberating on any of these four channels to influence target audiences: creating its own channels or getting the existent channels to cover the hacker group. For instance, the hacker group can create its own video channel (eg, via YouTube or a web TV application), create an Internet radio station, publish a magazine, or provide target audiences with a news bulletin (eg, an RSS or live feed). These channels can be filled with content; the type of content depends on the intended effects sought after by the hacker group (eg, deceptive, informative, degrading, etc.). These channels can be aimed at external communication (target groups) or internal communication (within the hacker group); in the latter case the channels may also stream instruction material.

Besides streaming its own content, the hacker group could also try to get existing media to cover the hacker group. Before being able to get the existing media to cover the hacker group, it is important to realize what these media cover, namely news or newsworthy information. Whether or not something is perceived as news or newsworthy information depends on a number of factors; the most relevant are timeliness, proximity, impact, rarity, conflict, and prominence. Timeliness comprises the fact that current issues are most interesting to read; proximity is about people's tendency to be more interested in local news than reports regarding issues far away; impact is about the potential influence content has on a person's life, the more impact, the more newsworthy the story; rarity expresses people's tendency to be more interested in unusual or unexpected storylines; conflict captures our drive to be more interested in news regarding conflict than news where everything is resolved in a peaceful manner; lastly, prominence expresses that we are more interested in famous people than in nonfamous people.

The content provided to new agencies, television channels, or magazines should fulfill one or more of the newsworthiness criteria. If content provided by the hacker group lacks all these, it is very unlikely that a reporter, journalist, or editor will pay attention to the story. The same goes for an operation aimed at getting exposure; if it does not fulfill the criteria, it will not get much attention in the media and within the target groups. For instance, when the hacker group wants exposure, it does not suffice to hack an account belonging to a "regular" employee of a company since it lacks prominence and impact. Hacking the account of a C-level official of a company, on the contrary, might spark attention for the hacker group.

There are multiple ways of reaching out to reporters, journalists, and editors. The formal way of reaching out to the conventional media is via press releases. Writing a proper, newsworthy press release takes time and some skill. After the press release is written, it has to be sent to the media; they often list an email address or phone number on their website for this purpose. There are other less-formal methods of getting the media's attention. For instance, establish direct contact with a reporter, journalist, or editor on social media (eg, Twitter or LinkedIn) and mention them in a specific post (eg, an "@" mention on Twitter) or send them a private message. Apart from that, the hacker group can decide to not contact the media but make the media come to them, for instance by focusing on getting maximum exposure for an operation by carrying out an operation against prominent targets (company C-level officials, celebrities, politicians, state organizations, etc.).

POSTOPERATION POSTURING

Cyber guerillas take action to further their goals by using asymmetry, flexibility, and stealth. Hacker groups combat larger actors by using these characteristics, but what will happen if they succeed at furthering their goal? Do these characteristics of cyber guerilla tactics still apply? This section focuses on the eventuality that the hacker group is successful: the goals are achieved and the raison d'être of the groups no longer exists or is not relevant any longer.

It is the most ideal situation for a hacker group: achieving their ultimate goal. There are many different goals, some more ambitious than others, but achieving them is generally a moment of euphoria. It is a moment of celebration while at the same time being one of the most dangerous moments in the history of the hacker group. This moment requires strong leadership making the other group members aware of the dangers of this moment. The group members may step to conclude that there are no more enemies and opponents; hence, they can be more lenient toward the characteristics of cyber guerilla tactics: asymmetry, mobility, and stealth. Even the most disciplined group members may step in the pitfall of thinking that there are no longer any threats for the hacker group.

Although the goals may be achieved, there are still many threats to the hacker group, most likely even more than before. The hacker group faces the risk of getting known due to their successful operations and resulting (media) attention. This will consequently result in attention from actors such as law enforcement agencies, other hacker groups, information security companies, forensic teams, intelligence agencies, information security researchers, etc. As such, instead of letting go of all the safeguards, the hacker group should be extra careful to not give away more information than needed (stealth), keep on the move virtually and physically (flexibility and not become over-confident and take on larger actors head-on (asymmetry). While heeding this warning, the hacker group can cast an eye on the horizon and discuss the future of the hacker group.

Having fulfilled all goals, the hacker group has three options: (1) take on a new opponent or issue area; (2) partially retire; or (3) fully retire. The first option, take on a new cause, is very similar to starting a hacker group all over. The group should (re)consider their goals and rethink their strategy for achieving these goals. It is vital to reassess the context, which comprises the societal context, the opponent/issue area, and the state of the hacker group (as described in Chapter 1). The context might have changed during or by virtue of the previous operations. To improve the hacker group, they should also critically evaluate previous goals, strategy, and operations. The feed-back derived from this evaluation should be integrated in the goals, strategy, and operations for the revamped hacker group.

Depending on the goals of the hacker group, it might be viable to only retire certain sections of the hacker group, for instance when the main operations have been executed and the goals partially attained but there is a chance that the opponent will recline into its previous behavior. Another situation could be that there is an opportunity to exploit success further by keeping a steady presence in (social) media. Hacker group leadership should make decisions designating certain sections of the hacker group to remain active and come up with an exit strategy for the sections which are no longer needed. The hacker group can remain a foothold in the media by keeping the accounts live and keep posting messages regarding the hacker group's successes, the opponent's loss, and the narrative of the hacker group for conducting the operations.

The transition from an active hacker group to a retired hacker group is fraught with dangers. If the hacker group decides to retire, many hacker group members will leave the group to join another group or leave "the scene" entirely. As a result of leaving the group, knowledge regarding the organization, operations, and tactics of the hacker group will disseminate beyond the control of hacker group leadership. This precarious situation for the hacker group requires a thought-through exit strategy.

The exit strategy should comprise a roadmap to dismantling the hacker group. This strategy should comprise a plan entailing the dismantlement of infrastructure (eg, who will do it, who will make sure all data are forensically wiped, etc.); guidelines regarding dissemination of knowledge regarding the group and its operations (eg, can members disclose their membership, can the operations be mentioned, etc.); dismantlement of accounts (eg, maintain social media, communication, and other accounts or dismantle them as well); and reevaluate the role of leadership (eg, will the nucleus keep in contact with members and each other).

Apart from that, hacker group leadership should prepare for the contingency that one of the hacker group members will leak information either voluntarily or involuntarily. To keep the other group members up to date regarding these kinds of hazards, the exit strategy should encompass a plan regarding safe ways of contacting retired group members. This is more difficult than during the active phase of the hacker group, since the leadership has to communicate without the use of the already dismantled infrastructure.

Chapter 4

Appendices

R. Gevers, M. Sprengers and J. van Haaster

■ INTRODUCTION

Che Guevara used his fourth chapter, appendices, to reflect on his endeavors in various guerillas around the globe. He used the appendices to analyze why some of the uprisings were successful and some were unsuccessful. He also described what to do when the guerillas succeed in ascertaining ultimate victory. Lastly, he used Chapter 4 to look at the future of guerilla warfare. We will use this chapter for a similar purpose: (1) to look at illustrative hacker groups and (2) the future of hacker groups.

ILLUSTRATIVE HACKER GROUPS (RICKEY GEVERS)

The previous chapters have focused on the conceptual basis of cyber guerilla (Chapter 1), hacker group composition (Chapter 2), and on conducting operations (Chapter 3). As mentioned in Chapter 1, cyber guerilla is an
amorphous phenomenon; it takes different forms depending on the context.
As there are too many different possible contingencies for a hacker group to
operate in, we have not prescribed modus operandi for specific situations.
In this chapter we will look at various illustrative hacker groups and assess
their performance using the guidelines we have sketched in this book. The
question we seek to answer in this section is, what illustrative hacker groups
have had success and could be used as example for potential cyber guerillas?

Anonymous

Probably one of the most known examples of a hacker group is Anonymous.
In a Guy Fawkes' (or V for Vendetta-like) fashion, nobody is anonymous
and yet potentially everybody is an Anon. Anonymous, as we know today,
started from the chaotic and disorganized bowels of the 4chan forums and
various other online communities. As mass groups of people were able to
communicate, share ideas, and "lulz," they could put numbers to use. In
many ways, Anonymous is a representation of a certain fringe part of the
Internet that tends to hide in the shade. As individuals, Anons are passionate
about their interests as any other person, but united—they become influence manifest. In time, these individuals would rally around causes, beginning with trolling Habbo hotel, to other people, and larger organizations
like the Church of Scientology. As things heated up, postchanology and so
on, it became political very quickly. Anonymous went from being simply a
fringe organization to a decentralized political organization supporting, for
instance, Wikileaks, wreaking havoc on the corporations trying to silence
Wikileaks and Assange's prosecution for sexual assault.

When looking at Anonymous their media organization especially stands out.
With only a handful of dedicated people Anonymous accounts flourished
on social media. These accounts were provided with content by members
or supporters and this information was constantly kept up to date via IRC
channels. As the information was constantly curated by members and their
supporters, the account became a trustworthy source for the latest news on
Anonymous's activities. Their self-regulation system was so effective that
at Anonymous's height, people would instantly believe anything on their
channels was probably true.

The greatest lesson learned from Anonymous is the value of media strategy and the use of external communication in a hacker group. Whether

purposefully or not, Anonymous is one of the few hacker groups that has successfully branded itself. Everybody can use their brand name, distinct style of video content, symbols, icons, etc. for whatever purpose. Some might say that the success of Anonymous eventually also led to its downfall. Although still being a very strong brand, as a consequence of the Anonymous brand being used and misused by any and everybody, Anonymous's credibility and trustworthiness has decreased. Threats, warnings, and operations are issued on a daily basis using the Anonymous branding; these become less and less effective.

LulzSec

Whereas Anonymous is the most well-known hacker group to the public, the LulzSec crew is probably one of the most famous and impactful (nonstate) hacker groups to ever have existed. This is primarily due to their consistent social media presence, technical skill, and target choices. Although the technical sophistication of operations was moderate, it ranged from low-level to very advanced attacks; all of the attacks did have huge impact on society. While conducting their operations in plain sights of the public, no LulzSec member was arrested. They remained illusive, almost invincible. The reason for them not being arrested later turned out to be that the leader of the group AnonymouSabu was already arrested and coerced into being an FBI informant.

The LulzSec crew factually consisted of two dedicated hackers: AnonymouSabu and Kayla. The others, Tflow, Topiary, Pwnsauce, and Avunit, were just along for the ride, nonetheless creating an extremely effective and strong group. Especially when we look at the LulzSec group the importance of dedicated leadership in a hacker group becomes apparent. Although the group itself always denied having a leader there was a very strong leader within the group: AnonymouSabu. The group consisted of individuals that all had their own area of expertise and character traits. For instance, some liked the media attention resulting from disclosing details of the attacks and claiming responsibility (ie, T-Flow). Others proved to have more politico-ideological incentives for conducting operations. These individuals, with differing motivations and incentives for engaging in operations, were able to pull off series of very high-profile attacks. The reason they were able to do so was strong leadership; the leader of the group was able to fulfill every member's ideological, material, or personal incentive for engaging in operations. He aligned their efforts when it mattered and as such was able to bring the group to unprecedented heights.

The next logical question is how AnonymouSabu could achieve such a feat. Irrespective of his role as an informant, he showcased great skill in molding the group into an effective crew and it would be very short-sighted not to learn lessons from his performance as leader. One of the elements contributing to his strong leadership role was that he was the person always online. AnonymouSabu was the person everybody talked to, but what is most important: he always talked back. He treated every individual with the same sort of respect. It was completely clear to everyone that AnonymouSabu was the "go-to" person and they could converse with him without him having a disdainful attitude or temper. That does not mean that he could not be very rude, but he only resorted to rudeness when forced by people that threatened him first. His own tweets expressed a clear political incentive and he used this channel to rally support for LulzSec and other movements that needed support. He chose to give this (moral) support only to carefully selected projects and not at random.

All of these aspects make AnonymouSabu one of the strongest leaders the hacker community has ever seen. This type of leader, who is charismatically, technically, and socially capable, is very rare. Once such a leader is present, however, he or she can lift the hacker group to unprecedented heights and contribute to movement success.

Jeremy Hammond—AntiSecurity

As we are mainly discussing groups in this chapter, we would like to highlight one individual as well, Jeremy Hammond. Jeremy has a long history of civil disobedience and showcases his ideological drives publicly, both online and offline.[a] Jeremy tried to join the LulzSec crew but eventually only took part in the AntiSecurity operations together with members of the LulzSec crew. Jeremy turned out to be a very skillful hacker; his problem was, however, that he had his own agenda. He never participated in the group and focused on his own goals.

Putting one's own goals before that of the hacker group ultimately corrupts the goals of the hacker group and potentially contaminates its reputation. Although his motivations for conducting operations were benign, he set out to cause as much havoc as possible, resulting in a lot of collateral damage. This collateral damage is something the hacker group should always strive to minimize. Individuals that have a mind-set like Jeremy could mean a lot to the hacker group but it should always be kept in mind that they could also completely destroy the incentive of the general public to support the hacker group.

---

[a]See for instance: https://www.youtube.com/watch?v=XvXk5xCM6PM

Cult of the Dead Cow "cDc"

This organization, which exists today, and has existed for close to 30 years, has had many famous members through its history. From researchers, phreakers, hackers, philosophers, and writers—this organization has made its impact on the Internet as it is today. Before "TOR," cDc had released BO2K (Back Orifice 2k)—which was originally a Remote Access Tool (trojan/malware)—allowing its users to convert infected machines into HTTP/HTTPS proxies for Chinese dissidents. They were also the organization to first engage in activities we have come to know as "hacktivism" going back to the year 2000 and perhaps even before. This group shows that a hacker group can directly contribute to oppression by putting their considerable technical skill at the disposal of the public.

Team TESO/ADM/w00w00/LSD-PL

These were groups made up of very talented individuals who excelled at security research, more specifically: reverse engineering and exploit developments. Most of these groups shared members, or collaborated together on research and ultimately changed the face of computer security. With their highly advanced exploits they were able to inspire young researchers with their new techniques, exploit development coding styles, and the speed of their research. These highly skilled individuals worked together very effectively because they were able to designate roles in the reverse engineering process. By doing so, they were able to produce and change the landscape of Internet security with every single release they posted to the Internet. These individuals have shown that although hackers may sometimes seem very individualistic, when working together they may rise to unprecedented heights. This also goes for the hacker group engaged in cyber guerilla.

Chaos Computer Club

The Chaos Computer Club resembles what is, according to the authors of this book, coming close to an optimal hacker group. They have extremely skilled members, a strong public persona, and many outlets to the media. The problem, however, is that the group lacks sufficient organization, coordination, and besides that they have a group of core members with a certain legendary aura around them. These "legends" are the people that have committed or achieved one very influential feat and as a result gain a sort of legend-like status. Less legendary or relatively new members deem everything they say to be the truth.

As "groupies" flock to them and they receive acclaim wherever they go, they alienate themselves from the real world. They do not receive proper feedback anymore and only have "yeasayers" around them causing them to become distant from the real world, real people, and real issues. Having one or more of these legend-like figures in the group can benefit the hacker group media-, knowledge- and leadershipwise. However, the hacker group will also risk becoming too narrow-sighted and follow the legend without considering whether it is a sensible course of action; this is the lesson that can be learned from the Chaos Computer Club.

Chinese APTs

Chinese APT groups are known because of their visibility. Examples of such groups are Mandiant's "APT1" or CrowdStrike's Putter Panda. The Chinese government never made any secret of their targets and goals; they are out there in the "open" hacking companies all over the world to collect intelligence to further the government's interests. The Chinese hacker groups are most likely responsible for the largest transfers of wealth in history, both in intellectual property and the monetary sense.

The reason for mentioning Chinese APT groups as illustrative to cyber guerillas is their successfulness. The modus operandi of the Chinese is very basic: stay persistent. They do so without investing excessively in stealth. The lesson that can be learned from this is that stealth, sometimes, can be a choice. If the hacker group has little to fear from the government or investigatory agencies, it could choose to operate in plain sight. Success can also be achieved if the hacker group operates out in the open. This emphasizes that the final goal should be of most importance and not the route toward it; the hacker group should consider all attack paths and not accept any course of action as the de facto standard.

Rebellious Rose

A hacker group presumably put together or supported by Iran and/or North Korea has been dubbed "Rebellious Rose" by the authors of this book. Either the group hires itself to both countries or both countries have together established this group. The most likely case is that they are state sponsored. The reason for highlighting them is that they are an example of a very effective and efficient group. The group itself is responsible for attacks on:

- Aug. 2012—Saudi Aramco
- Aug. 2012—RasGas
- Mar. 2013—DarkSeoul cyber attacks
- Feb. 2014—The Sands Casino
- Nov. 2014—Sony Pictures

What stands out with this group is their effectiveness. In most cases the whole attack did not last longer than 1 month and within this 1 month they were able to get into the company's network and eventually destroy the whole network and almost the whole company.

The toolset used by this group was always very basic and their skill level can be considered moderate. The group was, however, very successful in achieving its goals. The distinguishing feature of Rebellious Rose was their careful planning of the entire operation. A lot of operations fail or are not maximally effective as a consequence of a hacker group member becoming overly enthusiastic about the information found or foothold established and starts disclosing information too soon. This specific group always directly hit the company, maintained foothold, moved lateral, and finally extracted all information possible from the company. Once all information was extracted they rounded up the operation and started publicizing the attack. If you want to cause panic, sow fear, and impact the target maximally, it is essential to plan every aspect of the attack and make sure this plan is followed meticulously. This group has used this disciplined approach to operations in great effect; certain stages can be derived from their activities. We will describe these stages as illustrative examples of how to effectively manipulate a target actor. In this case we will dissect the attack on Sony Pictures.

Rebellious Rose first started to showcase their control of the network by slowly and visibly manipulating workstations within the company. They did this on such a scale that the attack was noticed fairly quickly by the employees and eventually the media. This method, destroying computers one by one, causes a lot of fear and panic for the system administrators and other supporting staff. At one point the support staff will realize they are not in control of the situation and start to shut down the company network to try and mitigate the attack. As a consequence of all systems or networks going down, the employees of the company become aware and start to realize that a very serious attack is going on. By the sheer number of workstations affected and consequently the employees realizing the severity of an attack, rumors start to spread and eventually the press will get ahold of this story.

To extend the fear and panic level even more, the group published about the internal network disclosing intricate details of the internal network. By doing so, the public became convinced that there was an actual attack taking place by the group and that the it was not another empty threat. Besides informing the public, these messages also stirred the information security companies, all looking to use this case to showcase their latest technical services, thereby bringing the incident under continuous attention from the public. The buzz created by the information security companies and their consultants regarding this incident provided the group with extra exposure. Often the tone and wording of these blogs (or simply their references to their security products) suggests that the attack could have been prevented (with their product easily), making the company's system administrators look like fools. This type of exposure degrades the target's already tarnished reputation even further.

In the last phase of the attack all information that had been stolen was slowly publicized. Most, if not all, company networks contain internal information which, when disclosed, is newsworthy. Once the target has made headlines due to the discovery of the compromise, there are plenty of reporters who want to have the latest information on the severity of the "hack." By slowly disclosing internal documents, the hacker group succeeded in extending the attention for the compromise from a few days to weeks.

This group showed that it does not require high-tech tools or extreme technical skill to be effective. This group showed that determination, adjoined with careful planning and discipline, can be equally effective. As such, they were able to remain undetected until the most optimal moment for exposure was reached. Once they disclosed their presence, they carried out a carefully staged media campaign to maximize their effect against the target. This group has shown to master the skills of undetected exfiltration as described in Chapter 2. They were able to get all of the data outside the company without getting noticed and once the information was out they were able to spread it to the general public, resulting in achieving their end-goal.

Anons Bataclan

In the aftermath of Islamic State's (IS) Nov. 2015 Paris attacks on a stadium, cafe, restaurants, and the Bataclan theater, a group using Anonymous branding was able to rally a huge amount of support for their operation (#OpParis) countering IS. They provided supporters with a number of guides, a NoobGuide on "hacking," a "reporter" guide on building a script searching for IS's Twitter accounts, and the "searcher" guide on creating a script on finding IS-affiliated websites. They generated target lists using the input from the searcher and reporter activities on Pastebin and Ghostbin for the supporters to use when selecting targets. Besides their efforts to accommodate supports, they were even able to create considerable (conventional) media attention. Considering these activities, #OpParis seemingly is a very successful operation. However, there are also lessons to be learned about being able to cope with the amount of media attention and number of supporters.

While being able to successfully create momentum by taking on a issue area in society (as described in Chapter 1), once they got attention they failed to adequately or in a timely manner translate this momentum into activities on a large scale. The days following the day of the attack (Nov. 13) thousands of supporters flocked to the IRC channels communicated over Twitter. Although having a channel for these nonmember supporters is a good thing to have; this channel should still be moderated by members. Moderating a channel can be daunting, especially when thousands of supporters are entering the channels. The IRC channel used for #OpParis quickly became chaotic and confusing for potential supporters. There were many different actors online, from reporters inquiring about #OpParis, opponents spamming the channels, supporters asking about how to contribute, to information security professionals and many others. The supporters entering the channel expected to receive guidance on how to contribute to #OpParis. Once inside the channel, however, it was very unclear what was expected of them. Different links to the "NoobGuide," "Reporter," and "Searcher" guides were posted on an irregular basis, some even linking to potentially unsafe domains. The target list on Ghostbin was frequently down, unclear whether it was due to a (distributed) denial of service or the amount of traffic generated by the supporters. All of the aforementioned elements illustrate that the group responsible for #OpParis was overwhelmed with the amount of supporters.

To adequately facilitate the supporters, the hacker group could have decided to use a different communication channel than IRC. While IRC may be the communication channel preferred by hacker group members, for common, nontechnical users it may come across as confusing and complicated. Instead, a website or forum would reduce the amount of supporters lost in IRC channels. This website should contain clear (visual) instructions to direct the supporter flow to different sections (eg, hacking, reporting, and searching) and associated FAQs. Besides that, clearly listing a point of contact for press inquiries on this forum or website would satisfy the reporters' need for information. Websites and forums allow for a more structured communication to many supporters since there is no direct way of communicating back. Thus, one of the lessons learned from #OpParis is that IRC as initial point of contact with large amounts of supporters is suboptimal; using more static means (websites or forums) would be more effective in this case.

FUTURE OF HACKER GROUPS

So far, this book has discussed the foundations (strategy, tactics, favorable and unfavorable terrain), activities (operations), and illustrated successful hacker groups and postoperation posturing. This chapter will now cast an eye on the horizon, how hacker groups will develop themselves. What are the consequences of these future developments for the activities presented in this book? Will they only affect the techniques, tools, and procedures or will they also have repercussions for the foundations of hacker groups?

Technologywise, despite some contingencies involving apocalyptical, blackout-like scenarios, the most likely future is an unprecedented increase in networking, use of information technology, and further integration of the physical, cognitive, and virtual domains. Very similar to developments in the last decade, the near future will envelop gradual proliferation of Internet access and associated technologies. Internet penetration will increase even in remote areas in this world. At the same time, the quality of connections (bandwidth and reliability) in already permeated areas will improve; as a result data production will increase even further.

Besides growing Internet access, the physical, cognitive, and virtual domains will increasingly intertwine. In the near future the use of virtual and augmented reality will increase both socially and professionally. The ability of manipulating these devices and content will become interesting for a wide variety of actors (state and nonstate). These virtual- and augmented reality devices offer a direct way of manipulating a person's perception of reality, as opposed to indirect manipulation via nudging, framing, and other influencing techniques.

Besides these first steps toward further human interaction with the virtual domain, we are seeing a gradual push toward more integrative "brain–machine interfaces." In the field of medicine (eg, prosthetics) and gaming industries (eg, nerve wear) there are increasing possibilities of integrating Man in its bodily form with machines' hardware and software. We currently are merely starting to consider the benefits of these prodigal technologies. Security, as with most new technologies, follows later. Brain–machine interaction opens up a new window for action for actors; these interfaces enable the direct manipulation of Man via the virtual domain. As the Internet itself, these technologies will be used for good, but also for malicious activities by states and nonstates. Thus, technologywise, Internet access and permeation will increase and certain technologies will change the way we interact with data, software, and hardware.

Societywise, we are well beyond our 1990s and 2000s naivety toward networking and information technology. Although we have spoken out against states' mass-surveillance programs, states will most likely tread even further in the virtual domain. We have seen a resurgence in the use of information as propaganda in the context of inter- and intrastate conflict (eg, Russia–Ukraine conflict). Violent nonstate actors have taken to the virtual battlefield as well; social media is being used to further their goals and to influence locally and globally. As mentioned in Chapter 1, all realms of online human interaction—whether it is multiplayer gaming or forum messaging—are becoming securitized and militarized.

This relatively new reality might lead to cynicism toward the Internet, networking, and information technologies. It is good, however, to realize that these developments have lead to great achievements as well. For instance, human interaction on an unprecedented scale, increasing knowledge production and consumption, unhindered exchange of ideas, concepts, and information, and an increase in trade and wealth. Although all of these elements are under pressure from those wishing to control the Internet and online human interaction, the Internet is generally one of the great and influential feats of Man. The Internet's securitization is not unique; there are many parallels with other technological developments. As we took to the skies, ventured into space, and crossed waters looking to explore or trade, in turn, this resulted in states and nonstates wanting to control these domains via regulations, rules, air forces, and navies. The same is happening with the Internet or the securitized alternative: cyberspace. All states are creating or pondering creating rules and regulations and forces able of controlling cyberspace.

Cyber guerillawise, in the light of these technological and societal developments, hacker groups are here to stay and will only increase in importance. As states and nonstates will extend their benign and malicious activities into cyberspace, many will benefit and many will be hurt. A range of actors will contest each other's control over cyberspace via all means available to them. Hacker groups will play an integral part in these conflicts, fighting alongside a state or other nonstate actor or opposing them. Future developments will influence the way cyber guerillas support or counter these actors. The following sections will reflect on the consequences for the concepts, tactics, techniques, and procedures put forward in Chapters 1–3.

Future of Chapter 1 (Jelle van Haaster)

Chapter 1 has discussed cyber guerilla objectives, strategy, and tactics. As these are on a high conceptual level; they will not change much as a consequence of future developments in networking and information technology. As mentioned in Chapter 1, before a strategy can be formulated it is essential for a hacker group to have a clear end-state or goal, understand oneself, the opposing actor(s), and the context in which the hacker group operates. The latter, context, will be affected most by future developments as the societal context will change by virtue of technological progress. With interconnection on an unprecedented scale, the context in which the hacker group operates becomes even more complex. There may be more opposing actors, conflicting hacker groups, supporting groups, and (target) audiences online. The hacker group should be able to traverse between these different actors and audiences; they should try to not alienate supporters and neutral actors, while at the same time combat opposing actors. Although this is not very different from the current situation, the complexity will increase significantly.

Chapter 1 further defined the three fundamental characteristics of cyber guerilla: asymmetry, mobility, and stealth. Future developments will have an impact on all three characteristics; the type of impact—beneficial or detrimental—will depend on the actual technological development. As more machines will come online, the hacker groups has more attack paths and potential infrastructure available to them, improving the asymmetric and mobile character of cyber guerilla. As more machines will come online and we will increasingly rely on soft- and hardware for human functions, security will also become an integral part in these systems—even more than it is now. New and improved access controls will make it harder for the hacker group to operate stealthily. However, as we have seen for the past decades, advances in defensive systems are rivaled by developments in the field of penetration testing tools and new ways of circumventing safeguards. Advances in defensive and offensive soft- and hardware will follow each other more rapidly. Hence the hacker group should follow these developments even more closely to prevent being compromised by new and improved intrusion detection or prevention systems.

Besides the ones mentioned, there are myriads of contingencies that can potentially impact the way cyber guerilla is waged on a tactical level. However, cyber guerilla is an amorphous concept, aimed at emphasizing the role individuals and groups can play on a stage now set by states and large organizations. The means for doing so, more than anything else, is a creative mind-set able of adapting to the circumstances at hand (as expressed in Chapter 2). Although future developments will have an impact on cyber guerilla, if the hacker group members have the proper mind-set, they will be able to make their cause heard.

Future of Chapter 2 (Rickey Gevers)

Chapter 2 described the moral fiber of the hacker required to fulfill the role of combatant and social reformer. Besides that, it also discussed the organization of the hacker group and the various disciplines within a hacker group. This section will expand on the potential effects of future developments on the ideological and organizational foundation of the hacker group.

Although many technological advances will take place, it is very likely that there will still be forms of injustice and oppression. The individual required to make a stand in the virtual domain will resemble the hacker fighting on the digital frontlines now. Hacker groups will still combat corrupt governments, resist the surveillance state, and generally fight against all forms of injustice or oppression. This will remain the same for the considerable future. Hence, the mind-set required for waging cyber guerilla will not change. Although the disciplines may change, the hacker group will still need to organize to make themselves heard and to influence issue areas in societies.

In the future, the Internet and its associated technologies may keep contributing to a better world, for instance a world without (or with less) corruption. For example, the banking system, one of the most influential and corrupt systems in the world, may be influenced by information technologies. Cryptocurrencies are gradually permeating societies; although not an adequate replacement for our current currency, digital currencies can be considered a beta version of the final system that will be created. These global payment systems illustrate the Internet's promise for creating new systems using interconnected communities, overarching sovereignty, territoriality, and nationality. Notwithstanding that the Internet will most likely (partially) fulfill its promise as catalyzator for the decline of the sovereign state, these states will try and grasp whatever power they have to impose controls on this domain. The Internet in the future will most likely be completely monitored and segmented. States will be able to shut down the Internet locally. However, as we are witnessing today, these developments will be met with tools, techniques, and procedures to counter the imposed controls. In sum, the battle for enjoying the Internet freely and anonymously will continue for the foreseeable future.

Future of Chapter 3 (Martijn Sprengers)

Chapter 3 has described the activities conducted by the hacker group members to attain their (end-)goals. These "operations" comprise the activities resulting in an effect that, when successful, may contribute to achieving the end-goal of the hacker group. Based on the operational lifecycle to perform digital attacks, specific tactics, techniques, and procedures and supporting tools were discussed. For future operations, it is important to understand that the more the society depends on interconnections, the higher the risk of disruption. As humans will struggle to cope with the shifts in technology, attackers can take advantage of people who do not fully understand the associated risks.

Technological advancements such as artificial intelligence, robotics, the Internet of Things, cryptocurrencies, and quantum computing will change the way we deal with data and computers. This also applies to the guerilla band as they too have to deal with this technological shift. An interesting paradox can be distinguished in our society: we have come to a point where citizens never had more means to obtain anonymity (such as TOR, encryption, and cryptocurrencies) and governments never had more means to monitor their citizens (such as cameras, usage of exploits, and communication interception). One of the consequences of this paradoxical situation is that governments will treat anyone who uses anonymity measures as suspicious, a trend already materializing in authoritarian countries. On the other hand, more and more citizens start embracing the notion of a shared economy, which highly depends on new technologies that use peer-to-peer–based sharing, over which governments have little control. This can be an advantage for the hacker group, as they can more easily blend into a peer-to-peer or shared economy than a more traditional, regulated, economy.

Apart from the social impact of rapid changes in technology, it will also impact the tactics, techniques, and tooling used by the guerilla band. In the short term, information security companies, law enforcement, and intelligence agencies will be able to perform more and better behavioral analysis. They will be able to collect much more (meta)data about Internet traffic: who is talking to whom, when, how much, and the medium. As metadata are a lot easier to store and analyze than data while being equally valuable to investigation, the increasing accumulation and analysis of metadata can complicate the conduct of operations by hacker groups and increase the risk of being profiled. On the other hand, the hacker group can use the ever-growing inventory of tooling and digital services to their advantage. As more technical specialisms will arise, the hacker group may not be able to incorporate or find all these specialisms within their group. As such, the future hacker group may resort to renting or purchasing specialist knowledge and services more than now.

In the long term, there is one important trend for operations: quantum computing. If a quantum computer can be built and become fully operational, this will have major impacts on human life. From a security perspective, many important encryption algorithms (such as asymmetric encryption algorithms) will be useless. However, history shows us that where humans can be beaten by technology, technology in turn can be beaten by humans. In the end, it is humans who make technology and humans make errors ...

Index

Printed in the United States
By Bookmasters